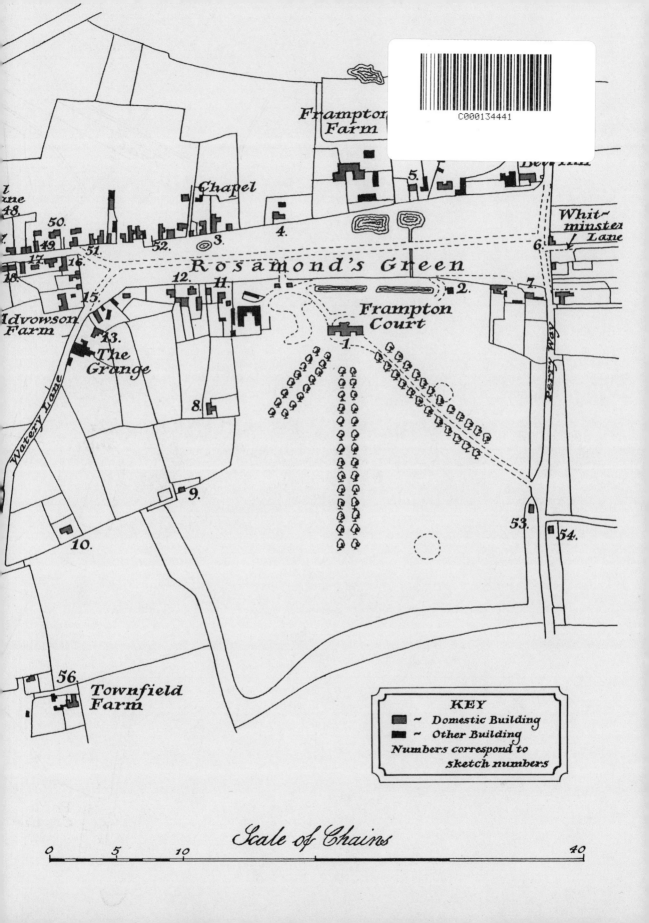

Frampton
Farm

Bell Hill

Chapel

5.

Whit~
minster
Lane

48.

50.

49.

3.

4.

52.

51.

17.

16.

6.

18.

Rosamond's Green

15.

12.

11.

2.

7.

Idvowson
Farm

13.
The
Grange

Frampton
Court

1.

Watery Lane

8.

Perry Way

9.

53.

54.

10.

56.

Townfield
Farm

KEY

~ Domestic Building

~ Other Building

Numbers correspond to
sketch numbers

Scale of Chains

0   5   10   40

FRAMPTON ON SEVERN

Portrait of a Victorian Village

FRAMPTON ON SEVERN

Portrait of a Victorian Village

Rose Spence

Phillimore

2000

Published by
PHILLIMORE & CO. LTD.
Shopwyke Manor Barn, Chichester, West Sussex

ISBN 1 86077 151 3

Printed and bound in Great Britain by
BIDDLES LTD.
Guildford, Surrey

Contents

Foreword vii
Acknowledgements viii
List of Subscribers ix

Introduction 1
Events in the 1860s 3
The Sketches 5

List of Sketches
  1 Frampton Court 7
  2 The Orangery 9
  3 The Green (west) 10
  4 The Green (west) 12
  5 The Green (west) 16
  6 Cottages at the top of the Green 20
  7 Frampton Cottage and Frampton Lodge, The Green (east) . . 22
  8 Fitcherbury 25
  9 The Shepherd's Cottage 26
 10 Alfred Draper's Cottage 27
 11 The Green (east) south of Frampton Court 28
 12 The Green (east) 32
 13 The Green (east) 34
 14 Advowsons 37
 15 Bottom of The Green 38
 16 Road leading to the Church 44
 17 The Street 46
 18 The Street (east) 48
 19 The Street (east) 50
 20 Buckholdt 52
 21 The Street looking south just after the Lychgate 54
 22 The Street (east) 56
 23 The Street (east) including the National School 60
 24 Vicarage Lane 68
 25 Vicarage Lane 70
 26 Park Corner 71
 27 The Vicarage 73
 28 The Street (east) after Vicarage Lane 75
 29 The Street (east) 77
 30 Bottom of The Street (east) 78
 31 Denfurlong Farm 80
 32 Church End House and Tanhouse Farm 82
 33 Field Farm (Splatt Lane) 84

34 Cottages by the Splatt Bridge 85
35 Splatt Bridge House 86
36 Cottage in Pound Lane 88
37 St Mary's Church 89
38 Church Court 90
39 Mrs. French's Farmyard 94
40 House just before Church Court, Church End 95
41 The Street (west) 96
42 The Old Thatch 97
43 The Street (west) 98
44 The Street (west) 100
45 The Street 102
46 Whittles Lane 104
47 The Street (west) 106
48 Woodbine Cottage 109
49 The Street (west) 110
50 Blenheim House 113
51 The Green (west) 114
52 The Green (west) 122
53 Entrance to Frampton Court from Perry Way 125
54 Perry Way 126
55 The Turnpike, Perry Way 127
56 Townfield Farm 128
57 Nastfield Farm 129
58 Parks Farm 130
59 Netherhills, Fromebridge 134
60 Fromebridge 136
61 Fromebridge 139
62 Walk Farm, Whitminster Lane 141
63 The Lake 142

Sources and Further Reading 146
Index 149

FOREWORD

As President of the Friends of Gloucestershire Archives I am well aware of the growing interest in local history and of the need to preserve our heritage for research.

I am therefore delighted that Henriette Clifford has made available her great aunt's sketch book from the 1860's because it is not only very interesting historically but it is also a delightful example of Victorian art as practised in the Country House of the day. Few villages in the Country are more idyllic than Frampton on Severn with its 14th Century Church and huge village green surrounded by thatched cottages and ancient manor. Many of the sketches show that little has changed thanks to the continuity of ownership by the Clifford family.

Rose Spence has captured the spirit of the village by recounting the ordinary and the extraordinary events throughout a decade of relative prosperity.

"Portrait of a Victorian Village" will be enjoyed far outside Frampton itself and is a valuable historic record of a truly rural community.

H W G ELWES

Lord-Lieutenant & Custos Rotulorum

Acknowledgements

The idea of producing this book came from the Rev. Dr. John Hunter of Frampton Congregational Church when we were discussing my interest in family history. My ancestors, the Hewletts, came to Frampton on Severn in the late 18th century from neighbouring Wheatenhurst (now Whitminster), and my great great great grandfather, Daniel Hewlett, built the chapel in Frampton in 1776. To help me discover exactly which properties my family had lived in John introduced me to Mrs. Henriette Clifford of Frampton Court, in whose possession is a small sketchbook containing drawings of virtually every house or cottage in the village in the mid-1860s. With the encouragement of the Clifford family and others in Frampton and beyond, *Portrait of a Victorian Village* has been written as a study of the village during the 1860s using the sketches. The project has been supported by Frampton on Severn Parish Council and forms part of the village's Millennium celebrations.

During the course of my research many people have helped me. To name them all would be impossible, but I would particularly like to thank the following: Mrs. Henriette Clifford (for allowing me to reproduce the sketches), Rollo and Janie Clifford, Tom Hewlett (my father, who patiently spent many hours researching for me), Hugh Conway-Jones (for his knowledge of the Gloucester and Berkeley Canal), Roger Vlitos (for sharing his research into the artists among the Clifford family), Geoff Gwatkin (for drawing the maps), Stephen Mills (for information regarding Fromebridge Mill), Pam Daw (whose research into Frampton proved most useful), Nigel Wills (who kindly allowed me access to the National School records), Rex Wood (for permitting me to reproduce a sketch of The Vicarage which belonged to his late wife), all those people who shared with me the history of their houses and families, and the staff at both the Gloucestershire Record Office and Gloucester Local Studies Library. To ensure historical accuracy I am grateful for the assistance of John Howe (Head of the School of History and Local Studies at the Cheltenham and Gloucester College of Higher Education).

Finally, mention must be made of the support of my family, who allowed me to research and write even when daily chores beckoned. I dedicate this book to my daughters, Heather and Nicola, without whose understanding it could never have been written.

List of Subscribers

Mrs. Lesley Aitchison (née Evans)
Queenie Aldridge
Carol Alexander
Fiona Alexander
William Alexander
Juliet Atherton
D.G. Attwell Esq.
R.L. Attwell Esq.
Mrs. Jean Awdas
Roger and Sandra Bagley
Betty Bailey
Ralph Bailey
Diane Baker (née Nicholls)
Prim Baker
Nigel Balchin
William Ballinger
Anne M. Barlow
C.M. and S.K. Bateman
Joan Bateman
Kevin Benn
Irene F. Berry
F.W. Birch
Paul Derek Birch
Tony (Calison) Bishop
Patrick Bisley
Sue Bonello
Harry and Mary Bowers
Dorothy Bradley
Rosa M. Bradley
Heather Brazington
Mrs. Beryl Brotherhood (née Coole)
Mike and Sheila Brown
Pat and Gina Bryan
Prof. and Mrs. W.E. Burcham
Lt. Cmdr. and Mrs. Godfrey de Lisle Bush
Mr. and Mrs. W.R. Butt
Muriel Cameron (née Hewlett)
Mr. David Campbell
Mr. Ken Campbell
Mrs. Mary Campbell
Ms. Tracy Campbell
Philip John Carter
Philip Cheesman
Diana le Clair
C.J.P. Clifford
Janie and Rollo Clifford
Mr. and Mrs. R.A. Clifford
Nanciette Clift
Dr. Cecil H. Clough
Alan and Jill Coker
Hugh Conway-Jones
L. Coole
Mr. and Mrs. H.C. Cursham
R. Dando
Richard Dando
Constance May Davenport
Val Davies
Reg Davis
Mrs. P. Daw

Dennis William Devereux
Mrs. Kathleen A. Dowle
Andrew Downton
Anne Downton
Lionel East
Antony Elliott
Mr. and Mrs. C. Estop
Mrs. Maude Evans
Mrs. Peggy Evans (née Phipps)
Cheryl Everall
John and Linda Farnhill
Frederick James Fear
Mr. and Mrs. M.J. Finigan
Tony and Nicola Forbes-Leith
Diana, Nigel and Rachel Foster
Dr. and Mrs. P.L. Furlong
Daphne Gardner
Mrs. Dorothy Gardner
Ray Gill
Wendy Margaret Goodman
David and Jo Granger
Louise Grant
Eileen Grassby
M. and K. Green
David and Pam Greenfield
Robert J. Haines
Dorothy Harrop
Pamela Hawker
Joan and John Hawkes
Jean Hawkins
Mr. A.G. Herbert
Mr. Eric Herbert
June Herd
Nancy Hewer
John Hewlett
Roy and Dorothie Hewlett
Thomas and Gwen Hewlett
Jane and Ian Hey
Kate Hilder
Geoffrey Hobbs and Malcolm Hobbs (Great
    Grandchildren of Thomas Hobbs, 1824)
Maree Hogan
Claire Hooke (Brinkworth)
Mrs. M.E. Hopkins
John and Milner Howe
Ken J. Hudd
John Hughes MBE
Lilaine Humphreys
Jonathan Charles Humphries (Grandson of Emily
    Margaret Brinkworth, 1886)
Ruth and Wally Hunt
John and Shirley Hunter
G. Hyden
Mr. and Mrs. G. James
Pamela Johnson (née Clarke)
B. Knight
Brian Knight
Lindsey Knightley (G. G. Granddaughter of Edwin
    Cox, 1850)

Valerie and Roger Lamb
Mr. S.G. Lander
Mr. and Mrs. B. Leach
Mr. and Mrs. S.C. Lee
Ray and Mary Lennox
Maureen Elizabeth Levens (Granddaughter of Emily
    Margaret Brinkworth, 1886)
Reverend and Mrs. Vernon Lidstone
Barbara and Alan Lloyd
Georgina Lock
Alan J.M. Lodge
John Loosley
Daniel Lord
Valerie Lord
The Lowder (née Daw) Families
Douglas Lund
Richard McHugh
Theresa Mahecha
Chris Marshall
Gerald Marshall
Kristin and Nigel Marshall
Martin P. Matthews
Jaime Maxwell-Grant
Margaret Melaney
E.C. and S.M. Merrett
Ivor D. Meyrick
Dr. Stephen and Elizabeth Mills
Mrs. Sheila Milne
John C. Milner
Bettina Mitchell
Russell Mitchell
Geoffrey Moore
Lucy Moore
Ms. E. Morphet
Mr. and Mrs. D.R.G. Morris
Mr. and Mrs. P.J. Mowatt
Sean Mowatt
Sarah Mulligan
Richard H.D. Myles and Michèle Price-Hunt
David Mynett
Geoffrey Mynett
Verna Mynett
Graham Nicholls
Robert and Eileen Nind
Mrs Shirley Norris
Diane Odell
Eileen, Michael, Rebecca and Jessica O'Gorman
Micky O'Gorman
Joseph Edward Orchard
J.G. Owen
Hilda Vera Page (Daughter of Emily Margaret
    Russell, née Brinkworth, 1885)
Edna Paisley (Brinkworth)
Terry Parker
David, Eunice and Ian Parkin
Joan E. Parks (née Aldridge)
Stephen G. Parsons
Anthea Peck (née Peacey)
D.H. Peck
Mary and Jerrold Pegrum
Jacky Pfister

Carole Phelps
Beryl Green Phillips
Anna and Simon Pinnington
D. Pockett
Cindy and Wayne Pratt
Sir Christopher Prevost, Bt.
C. Jonathan Price
R.L. Prout (Great grandson of Samuel Rowles,
    Buckholdt House)
Caroline and Nigel Pugh
Belinda Ricketts
Gill Rogers
Emily Margaret Russell (née Brinkworth)
Stephen J. Samuels
Ally and Geoff Shaw
Audrey Shepherd
Iris and Dave Shoebridge (ex Vicarage Lane)
Derek Shorthouse
Dot and Ron Smale
Rachel Smale
Mr. Bernard and Mrs. Joan Smith
M.E. Smith
Marie Smith (née Stevens)
Pat Smyth
Mrs. Tania South
Anne and Peter Spargo
Mike and Beth Sullivan
Mrs. Nora Bessie Summers (née Clifford)
Richard and Penny Sumsion
Diana and John Taylor
Margaret Taylor (Brinkworth)
Chris Temblett
Mr. and Mrs. John Thornell
Joan Tuck
Joan Tucker
Patrick and Pamela Turner
Pearl E. and Graham D. Underwood
J. Venn
Wg. Cdr. J.W. Vick
Trevor Vick
Roland and Betty Vielvoye
William Vincent
Paul Walkden
Graham and Emma Watson
Margaret and Les Watson, Tulip Cottage
Melva Watts
Gill and Dave Weatherburn
Maisie Weekes
Gilbert Wilcox
Mrs. Sally Ann Williams
Mrs. Sonya Williams
Ray and Moira Wilson
J.R. Wood (representing Mrs. M.E. Wood dec'd)
William F. Wood
Simon, Laura, Jack and Georgia Woodd
Gillian Woodhead
Mrs. B.F. Woodyard (née Law)
Mr. and Mrs. E. Worsley
Herbert and Betty Wyatt-Pickersgill
Lilian Young (née Herbert)
Eden Zoller

Introduction

> Frampton on Severn is a green little spot, cosily situated in the park-like scenery of the Eden of England. You feel, on approaching it, as if you had suddenly dropped into a corner of the world centuries older than our busy time; so strangely quiet is the place, and so noiselessly do the inhabitants move about, as if unwilling to break the sacred silence. It is one of the few villages nowadays that can boast a village green on which sheep and donkeys roam unmolested at their own sweet will.

Those words, written in 1874 by a person visiting the village for the first time, could still apply to Frampton today with its horses grazing on what is reputedly the longest village green in England. The approach to Frampton by the visitor of 1874 was via the Gloucester and Berkeley Canal (now called the Gloucester and Sharpness Canal) which runs between the village and the River Severn; for Frampton on Severn, despite its name, lies half a mile to the east of the river.

Nowadays, most reach Frampton by car. The narrow, straight road along Rosamund's Green, takes you past houses and cottages many centuries old. Ignoring the obvious signs of the present day, the scene looks very much as it would have done in the 19th century. Frampton Cottage, Frampton Lodge and Frampton Court to the east of The Green had been the principal homes of the Clifford family, whose connections with the village go back over 900 years.

Opposite Frampton Court, on the western side of The Green, is Manor Farm with its 16th-century wool barn. Parts of the house at Manor Farm are said to date back to 12th century and legend has it that 'Fair Rosamund' Clifford, the mistress of King Henry II was born there. According to some later accounts Rosamund was badly used by the King and spent the latter part of her life with the nuns at Godstow Abbey where she is buried. Her name, however, has lived on. The green was named after her in the mid-17th century and many local girls have been baptised Rosamund in her memory.

The 22-acre green, originally a marshy area until drained in 1731, has been a much-used facility over the years for travelling fairs, feasts and other celebrations. Cricket matches are played outside the *Bell Inn* at the top of The Green. Further down Rosamund's Green is Frampton's other public house, *The Three Horseshoes*, and beyond that the road narrows into The Street.

The Street boasts a wealth of different architectural styles in its housing, ranging from the 14th or 15th century until the present day. Many of the cottages and houses are built of Frampton brick, reminding us of a time when there were brickyards in the village.

A short way down The Street the lychgate tempts you along The Narles, a tree-lined path to St Mary's Church. Overlooking the lychgate is Buckholdt House, once the residence of a wealthy shipowner who could watch his vessels plying the canal from his upstairs windows. Further down The Street are Wild Goose Cottage and The Old Thatch, two of the oldest cottages in the village, and then the former National School (now a private house). After a sharp right-hand bend the road takes you to Church End, a cluster of cottages and the church. The road ends at the canal from where you can catch glimpses of the River Severn.

Apart from outlying farms, there are two other areas of Frampton which make up the old village. On the northern side of the Perry Way (B4071) are several older houses, and towards the Gloucester and Sharpness Canal is the area around Lake Lane, originally known as The Lake. Nearer to the A38 is the hamlet of Fromebridge (or Froombridge), notable for its mill. Comprising a few cottages and two farms, its history is traceable to Domesday Book, in which a mill was recorded worth 10 shillings.

During the 19th century the women of the Clifford family, like many others, engaged in the fashionable pastimes of drawing and painting. One of them, probably Mary Anne Clifford, set about the task of recording every house in Frampton and its occupants. It took her from 8 June until 9 October 1865 to produce most of the sketches, during which time she systematically worked her way around the village. Several others were added in the summer of 1866 and some are undated. Her pen and ink sketches allow us a unique insight into the village at that time, recording the scenes prior to any surviving photographs. Today most of the views are little altered, although some cottages have been demolished during the intervening years.

This book sets out to tell the stories of those families living in Frampton on Severn at the time of the sketches and what life was like for them in a Victorian village.

Events in the 1860s

In order to place the period studied in context it is useful to recognise some of the major events and characters of the 1850s and 1860s.

Because of the technological progress and creative energy displayed there, The Great Exhibition of 1851 had an enormous impact on England and her position as a world leader. Lasting from May until October it attracted 6 million visitors. The staggeringly spectacular Crystal Palace must have amazed all that went. Divided into four sections: raw materials, machinery, manufactured goods and fine arts, the Exhibition was a triumph for the Age of the Machine. The crowds looked on in wonder at machines for every kind of work, from folding envelopes to threshing corn.

Prince Albert, a dominant figure on the commission responsible for the Exhibition, was anxious that it should be seen by all classes of people, not just the privileged upper classes who normally attended such events. His success in uniting all classes, especially the workers, in their admiration for the industrial system, did much for the progress of the industrial revolution throughout the country.

The railways were able to offer transport to people across Great Britain and it is likely that some of the villagers from Frampton would have travelled to London amid great excitement to see the exhibits. They would probably have caught the Excursion Train from the nearby station of Stonehouse on the Great Western Railway line, spending one, two or four days in London, the fares in closed carriages ranging from 5 to 13 shillings.

The Exhibition profited from a combination of favourable circumstances coinciding with the start of a phase of great economic prosperity and social peace. The contrast with the chaos, conflict and famine of the 1840s could not have been larger. The English were almost the only people in Europe to have escaped the disturbing revolutions in the forties and the country was able to demonstrate to its neighbours that progress and welfare depended largely on individual effort and peace.

Thereafter, throughout the 1850s and 1860s, machines were employed to a greater degree, often replacing manual labour. In Frampton some were tempted by the idea of seeking their fortune or a better life in the industrial towns and many of the young men moved away from the village seeking both manual and clerical employment. Mechanisation, although relatively slow in coming to rural Gloucestershire, saw the gradual decline of many traditional trades. Farm labourers suffered more particularly in the 1870s from the effects of mechanisation coupled with several years of poor weather.

The families in Frampton in the 1860s were mainly long established in the village, and the decade could be considered as Frampton's heyday. The canal was thriving, bringing a constant stream of visitors to the village. Many of the traditional tradesmen had learned their crafts from previous generations of their families and the village was mostly self-sufficient. Goods were brought by local carriers from Gloucester, either along the canal, or by horse, cart or carriage. Business was frequently conducted in Gloucester or Stroud and the promotion of education among the working classes enabled young people to seek employment other than manual labour. Nevertheless, among the very poorest families there were still children who had never attended school and, until the later reforms in child labour, were expected to help their parents make a meagre living in all winds and weathers.

1859	Viscount Palmerston (Whig) became Prime Minister.
1860	Abraham Lincoln became President of the United States and the disintegration of the Union accelerated.
	The first south-north expedition across Australia started. Led by Robert Burke, it was completed in 1861.
1861	Frederick Walton invented linoleum.
	The American Civil War started. Richard Gatling invented the rapid-fire gun. Firing hundreds of rounds a minute, it was to increase greatly the loss of life in the American Civil War.
	Prince Albert, Queen Victoria's consort, died of typhoid aged 42.
	Mrs. Beeton's *Book of Household Management* and Charles Dickens' *Great Expectations* were published.
1862	The English explorer John Speke reached the source of the Nile in Lake Victoria.
1863	The London Underground (the first underground railway system in the world) was designed.
	The popular song *Clementine* by H.S. Thompson was first performed.
	The Prince of Wales' marriage to Alexandra of Denmark was marked by national celebrations.
	The Football Association was founded.
1864	The foundation stone of the pier at Weston-super-Mare was laid.
	The Clifton Suspension Bridge in Bristol was opened.
1865	William Booth started a mission in London that became the Salvation Army in 1878.
	The American Civil War ended having claimed *c*.618,000 lives. Slavery was abolished in the United States.
	Abraham Lincoln, President of the United States, was assassinated.
	The British Prime Minister, Viscount Palmerston, died aged 80. Earl Russell (Whig) took his place.
	Lewis Carroll's *Alice's Adventures in Wonderland* was published.
1866	Earl of Derby (Conservative) became Prime Minister.
	First instalment of Leo Tolstoy's *War and Peace* was published.
	The Atlantic Telegraph Cable was laid by Isambard Kingdom Brunel's ship *Great Eastern*.
1867	The first bicycle was produced.
	Joseph Lister published his theories on the antiseptic treatment of wounds. The need to sterilise medical instruments was slowly acknowledged.
	The *Blue Danube Waltz* by Johann Strauss was first performed.
1868	Christopher Sholes patented a typewriter and devised the 'QWERTY' layout still in use today.
	Flogging in the army in peacetime was abolished and the transportation of criminals ended.
	The Trades Union Congress was founded.
	Benjamin Disraeli (Conservative) and then William Gladstone (Whig) became Prime Minister.
1869	The *Cutty Sark* was launched.
	The Suez Canal was opened.
	The Anglican Church in Ireland was disestablished and disendowed.
	Henry Morgan Stanley was commissioned by the *New York Herald* to go to Africa to 'find' Livingstone, even though Livingstone was not considered lost or in any difficulty.
	The books *Lorna Doone* by R.D. Blackmore and Louisa May Alcott's *Little Women* were published.

Around the corner was Forster's Education Act (1870) which was a major step towards universal elementary education in England and Wales. It was not until 1880 that a further Act made elementary education compulsory, although fees were not finally abolished until 1891.

The Sketches

The little book of sketches measuring just 5½ by 3¼ inches (14cm x 8cm) is almost certainly the work of a member of the Clifford family. Exactly who drew them may remain a mystery as many of the female Cliffords were talented artists and the book is unsigned. The work of several of Henry Clifford Clifford's sisters and daughters is featured in Richard Mabey's book *The Frampton Flora* which depicts watercolours of the flowers and plants of the area. In this Mabey attributes the book of sketches to Catherine Clifford, Henry's fourth daughter, but gives no explanation for his reasoning.

No surviving diaries have been found nor any other papers which might shed light on the origins of the sketches. Clearly the sketches are an organised attempt to record the village in detail, and were possibly drawn for the ageing Henry Clifford Clifford to remind him how it looked and where everyone lived. Each property is shown in detail, from Frampton Court and the houses of the gentry, down to the most meagre peasant cottage. The artist shows no differentiation between classes and often includes the Christian names of the inhabitants.

It is most likely that the artist was one of the five daughters of Henry Clifford Clifford. Three of these, Elizabeth, Catherine and Constance, appear to be included as figures in the sketches. (Another, Charlotte, died in 1864 and a drawing of her grave is included in the book.) Edmund, Henry's son, is also shown. Mary Anne (1813-73), Henry Clifford Clifford's second daughter does not appear named in the sketches. When comparing the sketchbook with other signed drawings made by Mary Anne it is possible to recognise similarities in the style. Many of the other artistic members of the family had stopped painting and drawing long before the 1860s, but Mary Anne carried on, preferring to sketch rather than paint. Her caring nature leads one to feel that she was personally acquainted with all the villagers, no matter what their status. An obituary in the parish magazine describes her as one 'who had long lived in the affections of many a household in this parish; whose kindly glance and cheering words and ready sympathy will be missed by us all'. Her funeral marked a departure from the usual extravagances of mourning scarves, hatbands and gloves, for Mary Anne Clifford considered them to be too expensive for the poor to afford. It therefore seems to me that Mary Anne Clifford was the most likely artist.

Whoever drew the sketches showed an immense dedication to the task, for they were mainly completed over a four month period. The systematic way in which the village was drawn and the almost complete coverage of the dwellings and families have ensured that a visual record of the parish of Frampton on Severn in the mid-1860s has been preserved. It has been a privilege to look into the lives of the people depicted and to find out what the village was like all those years ago.

Whilst researching, a second book of twenty sketches was found. This belongs to the family of Sir Charles Prevost, who were resident in the village during the early 1890s. Many of the sketches are of exactly the same scenes that were drawn in the Clifford book, but they include some updating of the architecture reflecting the later Victorian period. Again the artist is not known but is thought to have been either one of Sir Charles Prevost's daughters or a friend of their family. The Prevost book contains a drawing of The Vicarage which was an important omission from the Clifford book and has therefore been reproduced in *Portrait of a Victorian Village*.

Throughout this book the sketches, which are mostly reproduced in a geographical sequence, have been numbered for ease of reference and indexing. These numbers have also been used on the two maps inside the front covers of this book. Because some of the original sketches show more dwellings than others, it has not always been possible to print them next to the appropriate text. The number of each sketch and its title has therefore also been included within the narrative. As virtually none of the cottages or houses bore names during the 1860s some present-day property names have been used to assist with identification.

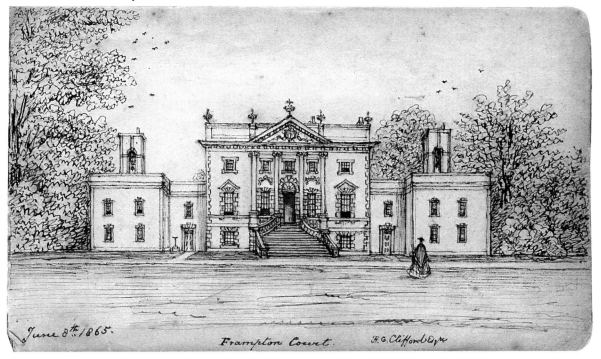

June 8th 1865. Frampton Court. F. C. Clifford Esqr

1 FRAMPTON COURT – 8 June 1865

Frampton Court was built between 1731 and 1733, possibly by John Strahan of Bristol, a pupil of Vanbrugh.

Henry Clifford Clifford

Henry Clifford Clifford (1785-1867) was for about sixty years Deputy Lieutenant of Gloucestershire and a Justice of the Peace. He inherited Frampton Court in 1817 upon the death of his father, Nathaniel Winchcombe, who had changed his name by Royal consent to Nathaniel Clifford to maintain the Clifford family name. After being educated at Eton and Trinity College, Cambridge, Henry married Elizabeth Wallington in 1808 and they had 11 children. He was widowed early, Elizabeth having died in 1838 when their youngest daughter was eleven.

Throughout his life, Henry was much loved by the villagers and was careful to see that the poor of the village did not suffer in times of hardship, providing them with free coals at Christmas and often allowing them to fall into arrears with the rents on their cottages. He owned virtually all the farms and many of the cottages and houses in Frampton and his agent, Mr. Vizard of Dursley, collected the rents half yearly in January and July. Maintenance on the properties was generally carried out by local tradesmen.

Henry Clifford Clifford's amiable qualities endeared him to his tenants and neighbours alike and he was particularly generous towards the upkeep of the National School, his charitable donations each year helping to provide the working-class children with the education their parents had often missed out on. Henry's daughters also showed their kindness and generosity towards the villagers and it is fair to say that during the time that Henry Clifford Clifford was lord of the manor the people of Frampton were relatively well cared for. The Cliffords took their responsibilities towards the people, buildings and land very seriously, and they were always ready to permit the use of their grounds for events such as a fête or feast.

The household at Frampton Court in the 1860s consisted of Henry, his five unmarried daughters, a butler, a footman, a housekeeper, two housemaids, a kitchenmaid and a stableboy. Like most employers, the Cliffords seem to have avoided taking on local girls as servants as it was generally thought that they might run home, draw 'followers' after them or convey gossip back to the community. Love sometimes blossomed 'below stairs' at Frampton Court and in 1856 Henry's butler had married the housemaid, although at the ages of 56 and 39 respectively they are unlikely to have caused much of a scandal. Other people employed at Frampton Court dwelt in cottages on the estate, such as the head gardener, William Jones, who lived in nearby Perry Way Lodge. The newspaper extract relates to the building now known as The Orangery.

The account illustrated opposite (probably from Henry's solicitor) of funeral expenses following the death of his eldest sister, Catherine Elizabeth Clifford, in 1863 gives some insight into the arrangements. There would have been separate bills for the coffin and the various items of clothing associated with mourning, and 'Servants' Goods' may well have referred to the purchase of suitable black clothing and the traditional scarves, hatbands and gloves.

FIRE AT FRAMPTON.—On Monday night a fire broke out in a large ancient building at Frampton Court, the residence of H. C. Clifford, Esq., and before it could be extinguished the left wing of the fine old edifice was destroyed, with its furniture and valuable shrubs and flowers. Shortly after three o'clock on Tuesday morning a messenger came in great haste into this city for the fire engines, and in a short time the fire brigade, with the Norwich and Phœnix engines, Mr. Superintendent Griffin, and five police constables, hastened to Frampton. On arriving there they found a large number of persons at work trying to put out the fire, and there being a good supply of water close to the building, they had succeeded in confining the fire to the left wing, where it first broke out, and by their exertions partially subdued the flames. The Norwich engine was soon got to work, and in a short time put out the remainder of the fire, but not before the whole of the left wing of this building, which was constructed many years since in the park, near to Frampton Court, for a billiard-room and a summer-house, but of late years has been used as a green-house, was destroyed, together with the furniture, fruit, seeds, and a large quantity of choice flowers and shrubs. Supdt. Griffin examined the building, and made enquiry to find out the origin of the fire, and found that the premises are constructed to be heated and warmed when required by two large stoves fixed in the wall, and open on the outside of the building. The walls are of great thickness, and hollow in the middle, through which pipes pass round the building, and join together in one chimney; near the top of the tower, about one o'clock on the afternoon of the previous day, James Hobbs, the under-gardener, lighted the fire in the stoves, and kept them burning during the afternoon. At seven o'clock Mr. Jones, the head-gardener, locked the doors, all appearing quite safe. At a quarter to one o'clock P.C. Eddolls, of the Whitminster Station, was on duty at Frampton, when he saw a light in the upper part of the building, and in a few seconds sparks came out of the window, followed by flames which burst through the roof; he at once raised an alarm, and in a short time 30 or 40 persons were on the spot, and by their exertions prevented the flames from destroying the whole building. Mr. Griffin discovered that the hot pipes for heating the room passed close to the deal boards and other timber in the roof; there can be no doubt but this fire was accidentally caused in this way, as the doors and premises were found locked as they were left by the gardener. The damage done is estimated at 400l. or 500l., and we are sorry to hear the property is uninsured.

Gloucester Journal, 30 November 1861

2   THE GREEN HOUSE (now THE ORANGERY) – 29 August 1860

This sketch pre-dates the fire and is likely to have been copied into the sketchbook from an earlier drawing.

The arrangements for Henry Clifford Clifford's own funeral four years later were on a larger scale and commensurate with his standing in the local community. The procession left Frampton Court for St Mary's Church at one o'clock in the following order: Twelve tenants on horseback; the bearers (six of Henry's workmen), two mourning coaches containing the family solicitor, the doctor and pall-bearers, the hearse, four coaches containing the mourners and ten private carriages.

As a magistrate, Henry was much respected both by the people of Frampton and throughout the county. He was described in the parish magazine as 'a fine specimen of the good old-fashioned English Country Gentleman'.

July 21. 1865.   *The Green.*

3 THE GREEN (WEST) – 21 July 1865

Stockelm Cottage

Stockelm Cottage formed part of the old workhouse buildings which closed in 1836.

Thomas Bennett

Thomas Bennett, a marble and stone mason, was born in Frampton *c.*1807, the son of George Bennett, also a mason. He bought Stockelm Cottage sometime before 1841 and lived there until his death in 1883. He married Sarah Young from Flaxley in 1833, whose elderly mother was a proprietor of houses and land, so Thomas appears to have married well. In later life he was appointed as one of the Overseers of the Poor and a Norwich Union Fire Insurance Society agent. As a stone mason his work can be found in local churches notably at Whitminster, Frampton and Moreton Valence.

He was one of the enumerators for the 1861 census, collecting the details of everyone living on the western side of The Green and The Street. The number of people in Frampton had changed little since the previous census (983 in 1861 compared with 994 in 1851), but the 'enumerators observed that where ten years ago they had met with trouble and difficulty in their task, they now found a civil and hospitable welcome and a cheerful readiness to lighten their labours'.

Sarah Bennett died in 1878 and four years later Thomas married again, to Sarah Agnes Godfrey, a spinster of almost fifty years. They were to have but little time together, for Thomas died 11 months later 'after a painful illness, borne with Christian fortitude'. Thomas was anxious that both his children and new wife should be provided for in his will which was written three days before his death when he was too feeble to sign his name. It was witnessed by two local surgeons.

Frederick William, his eldest son, had followed his father's trade and inherited both his

Thomas Bennett. Mrs Sumners. Mr Horner. Post Office

stock and tools as well as Stockelm Cottage on the proviso that Sarah, his widow, be allowed to live there rent free for six months. His younger son, Edward Young Bennett, was bequeathed the 'casks in the cellar'. The house had been well furnished in Thomas's time with, amongst other things an eight-day clock, two dining tables (of oak and mahogany) and a mahogany sofa.

Portland Place

John Sumner

John Sumner (*c*.1790-1872) was born in Bristol, but his family later moved to Frampton. Whilst living in Portland Place John Sumner was a chemist and druggist, stationer and stamp distributor and he sold the parish magazine from its inception in 1861 until a couple of months before his death. He stocked a range of pills, powders and tinctures, dispensing from the many bottles and jars that would have been displayed around his shop. He would also have sold the popular pills and oils which claimed to improve the well-being of the person, and live medicinal leeches, kept in specially made leech jars, which were used to bleed people.

Although unmarried, John Sumner was very conscious of his responsibilities within his family, and his will gives an idea of his straightforward principles. He desired that his body be decently buried with or near to the remains of his 'dear parents' in Frampton churchyard. He was anxious that any debts should be settled as quickly as possible after his death and left everything, including musical instruments and music, furniture, books, linen and plate, together with some modest investments, to his widowed sister Sophia, who was living with him. He was particular to mention that Sophia must not sell or destroy the pictures and collections in the parlour and other rooms, but should keep them in the memory of him and their parents.

John Sumner's important place in the village is emphasised by there being a note of the sale of his effects at the *Bell Inn* in the National School's logbook.

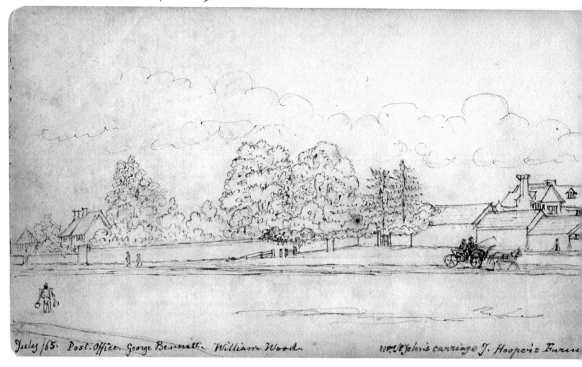

July /65. Post Office. George Bennett. William Wood. Mr. St John's carriage. J. Hooper's Farm.

William Horner

William Horner (*c.*1786–1867) was also born in Bristol. He was an attorney and lived in Whitminster in the 1840s, but by 1851 William and his wife Amelia were living in the northerly part of Portland Place. He owned properties in the nearby villages of Wheatenhurst (Whitminster) and Eastington. William was later an agent of the Norwich Union Fire Insurance Society and was an active member of the local Literary and Mechanics' Institute being its president on more than one occasion.

Following William's death Amelia Horner lodged with Thomas Bennett at nearby Stockelm Cottage. There was an auction of William's 'genteel household furniture' and Thomas Bennett was bequeathed ten pounds in his will for 'his trouble in being executor'. (Thomas was fortunate, for often the executor's work went unrewarded save for any expenses incurred.) Amelia died in 1881.

4 THE GREEN (WEST) – July 1865

Manor Farm Cottages

The northerly part was possibly constructed in the 15th century and was probably originally a small hall house. The building was enlarged to the south in the 17th century and for a while remained as one dwelling.

George Bennett

George Bennett (1805-78) was born in Frampton. He married twice, his first wife having died early in life, leaving him with three young children to bring up. In 1841 he was living in the

George Workman

southerly part of Manor Farm Cottages with his mother, two brothers, three children and a lodger. The Bennetts were a family of stone masons, and the cottage was later occupied by George's son John, a monumental mason.

Presumably, at the time of the sketch the garden contained many fruit trees and bushes, since George won several prizes between 1864 and 1867 for his fruit in the Frampton and Fretherne Cottage Gardeners' Society shows. These were large annual events held alternately in each of the villages and attracted entries from both cottagers and professional gardeners. In Frampton a marquee was erected in a field adjoining The Vicarage and the show commenced at two o'clock, when judging was complete. The Gloucester Artillery and Engineers' Band played throughout the afternoon and the grounds were soon filled with visitors admiring the wide variety of fruit, vegetables and flowers on display. In 1863 there was even a pineapple, grown in the hothouse of Sir Lionel Darell of Fretherne Court, exhibited.

Two years before his death, after a long and faithful service of almost fifty years, George Bennett resigned as postmaster to the great regret of all in the village. He had succeeded his mother Nancy, who had been postmistress working from the same cottage. The hours had been long, with letters arriving each morning from Stonehouse and being despatched in the late afternoon. In 1864 the Post Office had opened a Savings Bank providing many of the poorer villagers with the opportunity to manage their meagre earnings more effectively.

George's daughter, who had managed the telegraph amongst other post office work, had hoped to take over from her father. However, according to the parish magazine, the Postmaster General objected to the appointment 'on the grounds of the premises not being suitable'. After several months, with nothing having been done to upgrade the premises, the post office was moved to a nearby shop which was then owned by Nathaniel Stockham.

William Wood

William Wood lived with his wife Sarah and their two children, William and Emma, in the much older northerly part of Manor Farm Cottages. Born in Dursley c.1814, he probably arrived in Frampton sometime between 1841 and 1851. Like many carpenters and wheelwrights, both William, and later his son, also made coffins. Usually the production of these would have been a family affair, with the wife making shrouds and death pillows that had carefully serrated edges and were filled with wood shavings.

Mrs. St John

Mrs. St John, shown in the carriage, was the wife of the vicar of Frampton. The Rev. St John was a much loved and respected clergyman who served the parish from 1853 until 1881.

Manor Farm

Traditionally the birthplace of the mistress of Henry II, 'Fair Rosamund' Clifford (who died c.1176), it is possible that the oldest part of the house dates from that time. Much of the property was built in the early 16th century, although there were some later additions during the next one hundred years. The barn was probably built for the storage of wool in the 16th century. Manor Farm remains in the ownership of the Clifford family today.

John Hooper

At the beginning of the 1860s the tenant farmer was Joseph Barrett. After 34 years at what was then known as Frampton Farm he retired following an auction of his farming stock and goods.

John Hooper, born c.1815 in Redmarley, Worcestershire, took over the running of Frampton Farm at Lady Day (25 March) 1864 with his wife Ann and five grown up children, just a year before the sketch was drawn. The farm extended across the Gloucester and Berkeley Canal into the neighbouring parish of Fretherne and as far as the River Severn. In 1867 Henry Clifford Clifford made an allowance of £22 16s. 0d. against an annual rent of £585 'in respect of land destroyed and injured by the tides' during the winter of 1865-6. The Severn's narrow estuary causes the tide to move swiftly up the river in the form of a steep-fronted wave several times a year. Known as the Severn Bore, the phenomenon has drawn crowds of onlookers throughout the centuries, and can cause damage to the soft banks. (In September 1869 most of the pupils were late for morning

THE FARM, FRAMPTON-ON-SEVERN, GLOUCESTERSHIRE.

TO BE SOLD BY AUCTION,

By JAMES KARN,

On the above FARM, on TUESDAY next, the 10th day of November, 1863,—

THE whole of the LIVE and DEAD STOCK, HAY, CLOVER, CORN and STRAW, AGRICULTURAL IMPLEMENTS, and other Effects, the property of Mr. JOSEPH BARRETT, who is giving up the Farm; comprising 14 very useful in-season cows, 2 barrens, 7 in-season heifers, 15 yearling heifers, 8 yearling steers, yearling bull, 53 ewe and wether lambs, 10 ewes, sow and 7 pigs, sow and 6 pigs, hilt in farrow, 4 strong store pigs and 4 porkers, 16 cart and half-bred horses and colts, 5 ricks of wheat, 2 ricks of beans, 2 ricks of peas, 2 ricks and mow of barley, 6 ricks of prime meadow hay and clover, also the whole of the agricultural implements, and other effects, the particulars of which are now circulated in posted catalogues, and others may be had at the Sale.

N.B.—Any Person having any DEMAND on Mr. BARRETT are requested to forward particulars of the same to the Auctioneer, Bear Hotel, Newnham, immediately.

The whole of the Clover, half the Meadow Hay and Straw, will be Sold to go off the Premises.

Luncheon at Eleven o'clock, and Sale positively at Twelve o'clock to a minute.

Gloucester Journal, 7 November 1863

STEALING TREES.— *William Stapleton*, a gardener, and parish clerk of Whitminster, was brought up in custody charged with stealing 46 raspberry trees, the property of Mr. John Hooper, farmer, of Frampton-on-Severn. The prosecutor stated that on the 7th instant he employed the prisoner to work in his garden, and told him not to destroy or take away any of the raspberry canes as he wanted them. In the evening he saw prisoner carry out of the garden the trees produced, and conceal them. He watched him, and on the prisoner leaving to go home he observed him carry off the trees, and followed him and took them from him. The prisoner admitted taking the trees, but said he had been allowed to have trees before.

A good character was given him, and the prosecutor said he did not press for a severe punishment.

The Bench remarked that it was very bad for the prisoner to rob his master after being told not to remove the trees. Ordered to pay 1s. 6d. damage, and fined 1l. with 4s. 6d. costs.

FILIAL AFFECTION. — *Peter Alder*, of Harescomb, was

Gloucester Journal, 10 December 1864

WHITMINSTER. — PETTY SESSION, *Thursday*. —(Before H. H. Wilton and J. Grey, Esqrs., and the Rev. . Peters.)—Charles Davis, labourer, of Saul, was summoned for stealing, on the 17th inst., 21 growing turnips, the property of Mr. John Hooper, farmer, of Frampton. He admitted the offence, and Mr. Hooper said he had only brought forward the case as a caution. The magistrates said they hoped it would prove a caution, and fined the man 2s. 6d. and costs.

EASTINGTON.—Two sermons were preached in

Gloucester Chronicle, 30 October 1869

lessons at the National School having witnessed a particularly spectacular bore.)

John Hooper quickly established himself in local life, holding the position of waywarden for many years, an office that had been previously held by Joseph Barrett. The waywarden was elected annually and represented the Parish on the local District Highway Board. John Hooper also took an interest in St Mary's Church, proposing at a meeting of the Vestry in 1870, that the churchwardens should apply for a faculty in respect of the intended church alterations. His Christian principles led him to seek justice when necessary, but at the same time forgiveness.

The Red House

The Red House was built in the mid- to late 17th century. The present wooden dovecote set on the front wall façade between the floors is a 20th-century addition.

George Workman

George Workman was born in Frampton in 1820 and followed his father into the family trade of glazier, extending his occupation to include plumber and painter. One of his prime tasks in the village was the maintenance of its many pumps. Typically he charged 3s. 6d. for providing and fitting a new bucket and leathers for a lifting pump during the 1860s.

Sometime after his father died in 1841 he married Susan from neighbouring Worcestershire, and they moved into The Red House, a property owned by Henry Clifford Clifford for whom George regularly worked. After their children had grown up, George and Susan took lodgers among whom were the curate of Saul and Moreton Valence, a schoolmaster and a retired farmer. Like many women in the village, Susan would have spent most of her day at home seeing to the household chores. 'Wash day', as the name suggests, was a lengthy business with the work often extending over several days and evenings. Coloureds and whites were washed separately, the whites being carefully soaked and boiled to ensure their cleanliness. Preparing and cooking meals, housework and attending to the fires all took considerable amounts of time and it is possible that Susan employed a young girl to help her.

August 5th 1865.   Mrs Russell.

5   THE GREEN (WEST) – 5 August 1865

Russell House

The original parts of Russell House were probably built in the early 18th century. There have been 19th-and 20th-century additions, principally to the rear of the property.

Ann Russell

William Russell (*c.*1809-57) was born in Southwark, his wife Ann coming from Plymouth. According to the Poor Rates records they lived in this house in 1836, and the census of 1841 indicates that Ann's mother and sister were there too. Despite being considered among Frampton's gentry, the Russell's house did not have a water closet, William and Ann Russell having only 'the usual common privy and vault in the garden' according to correspondence in the Clifford archives.

In 1837 William Russell had copied out the register of Frampton's Congregational Chapel (for at the onset of civil registration all nonconformist registers were supposed to be deposited with the Registrar General, although in practice not all were) where he appears to have been a regular worshipper.

William managed his affairs in a prudent manner that included taking out a life insurance policy in 1834 with the Pelican Assurance Office in London. He made his will a year later leaving everything to Ann, who lived in Russell House until her death in 1882.

Thomas Farm. Bell Inn.

The Top Shop

This was probably built between 1780 and 1820; the bay shop windows being a 19th-century addition.
At the time of the sketch this property may have been unoccupied because there is no captioning. Earlier in the century it had been the home of William Richardson (minister of the chapel) and his wife Elizabeth. After William's death in 1847 the house was occupied by their niece, also named Elizabeth. She died in 1859 but her household accounts' books and details of her funeral expenses survive. It is interesting to note that because there was no graveyard at the chapel members were buried in the churchyard at Frampton. Her coffin and tombstone were made by Edward Hewlett and Edward Morgan respectively, and the funeral was furnished by Samuel Ward. All three were nonconformist villagers.

Major John Henry St John, who was possibly the brother of the vicar, lived in the property with his wife Margaret and their three young sons from *c.*1860.

Enoch Hill and his family arrived in Frampton *c.*1868 and were probably the first people to run a shop from the premises. A grocer and draper from Cam, Enoch had spent the first few years of his married life in Manchester. However, the family soon established themselves as part of the local village scene and were staunch supporters of the church and National School. From 1872 onwards the parish magazine was sold from the shop, and the vicar suggested that everyone might like to buy an evening paper entitled the *Sun* priced at one farthing a copy from Mr. Hill. Copies of religious services were also on sale at the more expensive price of one penny each.

Bell Inn

There was an inn on this site in 1740, but the present building dates from the late 18th or early 19th century.

Thomas Karn

Thomas Karn took over the running of the *Bell Inn* from his father, also named Thomas. Born in Cambridge or Slimbridge *c.*1808, Thomas never married and at first his sister and her husband appear to have lived with him together with various servants, but later he employed a housekeeper.

Thomas Karn also farmed 30 acres of land. He was a popular man, often described as 'Host Karn' in contemporary newspaper reports, and the *Bell Inn* was widely used for a variety of important occasions including inquests. Auctions of stock, property and household effects were run by Thomas' brother James Karn, a well-known auctioneer who lived in Newnham. It was also a Posting House, ideally situated on a turnpike road at the end of the village. Thomas Karn kept a fly (a light one-horse covered carriage) which he let out on hire, the cost to Stonehouse Station being 5 shillings.

Rents from the tenants of Henry Clifford Clifford were collected at the *Bell Inn* twice a year at 12 noon, after which those who had paid were treated to a 'Rent Dinner'.

FRAMPTON-ON-SEVERN.—The gale raged here with great violence. Houses were partially unroofed, chimney stack blown down, and some of the finest trees in the locality torn up by the roots. At the Bell Inn, the chimney stack fell through the roof into the bedroom occupied by the housekeeper and the servant maid. A massive cross-beam in the ceiling broke the fall, or the inmates would probably have been killed. In the park of H. C. Clifford, Esq. twelve elm trees were prostrated.

Gloucester Journal, 23 February 1861

SUDDEN DEATH.—On Tuesday an inquest was held at the Bell Inn, Frampton-on-Severn, by Mr Ball, on the body of Joseph Clarke, aged 40, who died suddenly on the previous Saturday. From the evidence it seems that on Friday night deceased, who lodged at the Bell Inn, went to bed in his usual good health and spirits, and about five o'clock next morning was heard by a man who slept in the room moaning; assistance was obtained by the landlord who tried to administer some brandy, but deceased could not take it. Messrs Walters and Watts quickly attended, but deceased did not rally, and died at eleven o'clock the same day. The cause of death was believed to be a fit of apoplexy. The jury returned a verdict accordingly.

Gloucester Journal, 23 January 1864

Thomas Karn's retirement from the *Bell Inn* in 1875 was marked by the presentation of a gold watch from his friends and neighbours in the village. He had lived there for 56 years.

6 COTTAGES AT THE TOP OF THE GREEN – 7 August 1865

Elm Tree Cottage

This detached corner cottage probably dates to the early 17th century.

Joseph Priday

Joseph Priday (*c.*1836–96) was born in Standish and arrived in Frampton between 1861 and 1865. He married Sarah Price, a widow several years his senior, in 1869. Joseph paid an annual rental of 10 guineas to Henry Clifford Clifford and lived in Elm Tree Cottage probably until his death.

As a carpenter and wheelwright he would have learnt his trade through being apprenticed, with the skills required having been passed on to him, for there was little in the way of drawings and books for such men to work from. It is likely that Joseph Priday would have made and mended farm wagons and carts, as well as wheels for other items, and he would have needed the services of one of the village's blacksmiths to fit the iron tyre at the end of the process. The making of a wheel was an exacting craft and different woods were used for the various components. The nave (or centre) of the wheel was made of elm, the spokes were of cleft heart of oak (the cleaving being done to preserve the strength needed in the longitudinal grain of the wood which might otherwise be damaged if sawn), and the felloes (sections forming the rim of the wheel) were of ash, elm or beech.

Top O' the Green

William Higgins

In 1861 this house was occupied by Mrs. Elizabeth Hewlett (a widow), her stepson William Hewlett, William Higgins and his family and the family of Samuel Mills, a photographic artist from Dudley, Worcs. Born *c.*1824 at Elmore, William Higgins had married Elizabeth Hewlett's niece. William, a farmer of between 6 and 8 acres of land, lived in this house until the mid–1870s when he could no longer afford the rent because of the repeated failure of his crops.

Elizabeth Hewlett had died on 7 May 1865. She and her late husband Richard had farmed at Church Farm earlier in the century and his grave can be found just to the right of the main door to the parish church. A shopkeeper in later years, Elizabeth had lived well in what was considered one of the better houses in Frampton, paying an annual rent to Henry Clifford Clifford of £16 0s. 0d. The notice (right) details the sale of her extensive household goods.

FRAMPTON-ON-SEVERN.

TO BE SOLD BY AUCTION.

By HUMPHRYS and SON,

Without reserve, on the PREMISES, on Thursday, January 11th, 1866, commencing punctually at one o'clock,—

THE Neat HOUSEHOLD FURNITURE and other Effects, late the property of Mrs. ELIZABETH HEWLETT; comprising four-post, half-tester, and other bedsteads; palliasses, beds, bolsters, and pillows; mahogany, oak, and painted chests of drawers; mahogany and painted washing and dressing tables; oak linen chest, swing dressing glasses, towel horses, blankets, linen, bedroom chairs, 2 couches, mahogany and oak dining, Pembroke, work, and other tables; 2 easy chairs, covered with leather; carpets, mahogany frame and other chairs; 30-hour clock and case; alarum clock, books, tea trays, and waiters; oak writing desk, glass, dinner ware, kitchen requisites, fenders and fire irons; and a quantity of other useful Effects.

Gloucester Journal, 6 January 1866

6 Cottages at the top of the Green

August 7th/85. Cottages at the top of the Green. *Priday.* Higgins

William Barradell

An agricultural labourer, William Barradell was born in Upton St Leonards *c*.1835. He and his Oxfordshire-born wife Mary occupied this property throughout the 1860s.

William Pick

William Pick (*c*.1840-98) was an ostler (stableman) who worked during the 1860s and early 1870s at the *Bell Inn*. Sometimes he had to stay the night at work to look after the horses, even though he lived within sight of the inn. The sketch reveals what appears to be stabling at the side of William Pick's house which may have been used by the *Bell*.

The son of Joseph Pick, a sawyer who lived on The Green (east) near the lane to Fitcherbury, William had been born in North Nibley. He married Jane and they had six children between 1863 and 1871. The family moved to the *George Hotel* at Frocester early in 1872 where William did well for himself, running the hotel until his death.

Northend House

Originally built in the late 18th or early 19th century together with The Old Post Office.

Mary Ann Hill

Probably the wife of George Hill, a waterman, Mary Ann was born in Frampton *c*.1847. Their daughter Ellen was born *c*.1865.

Barradell.   William Pick.   Hill   Andrews.

The Old Post Office

Joseph and William Andrews

Joseph Andrews, a blacksmith born *c.*1811 in Whitminster, came to this house from Fromebridge with his family during the 1850s. His son William (born *c.*1836 in Frampton) was a waterman. William married Ann, who came from Slimbridge, sometime between 1861 and 1871 and it may have been at that time that Joseph and his wife Mary Ann moved to a cottage in The Street (east), leaving the newlyweds to live in the family home.

7   FRAMPTON COTTAGE AND FRAMPTON LODGE, THE GREEN (EAST)
– 8 August 1865

Frampton Cottage

Henry James Clifford

Henry James Clifford had only lived in Frampton Cottage for a short time when this sketch was drawn just a few days after his marriage to Annie Frances Green, the daughter of the Rector of St Aldate's, Gloucester and Chaplain to the Bishop. The wedding, on 26 July 1865, had been a splendid occasion conducted by the Bishop of Gloucester who was assisted by the Rev. Edmund Clifford, an uncle of the bridegroom and curate of the neighbouring parish of Fretherne. In 1867, upon the death of his grandfather Henry Clifford Clifford, Henry James Clifford inherited Frampton Court and the Clifford family estate.

H. J. Clifford. Frampton Cottage.

Henry James, born in Frampton in 1840, was a magistrate but, unlike his grandfather, he was not always totally committed to his responsibilities within the village and local community. His father, Henry John, had died when Henry James was only 12, and it seems likely that Henry Clifford Clifford would have then set about the task of teaching his grandson how to run the estate and care for the villagers. Nevertheless, when Henry Clifford Clifford died it was the Rev. Edmund Clifford (H.C. Clifford's son) who generally took charge of estate and family matters. In his lengthy correspondence to Mr. Vizard of Dursley (agent to the Cliffords), Edmund mentioned on a number of occasions that he could not progress matters as 'Harry' (Henry James) was away either travelling or hunting: 'Harry being out hunting so often, I have been unable to get hold of him.' A man of seemingly endless patience and forgiveness, Edmund was left to deal with some very serious problems.

Firstly, Frampton Court was greatly in need of repairs and it seemed inevitable that it would either have to be sold or rented out, as the family could not afford its upkeep. Within just a few months of Henry Clifford Clifford's death his unmarried daughters had moved out to Dursley, and to Edmund's evident relief Frampton Court was let: 'Harry has let the Court to Captain Chapman. Hurra!'

Secondly, Henry James' lifestyle caused additional financial burdens. He was frequently away from Frampton travelling throughout Britain and Europe, notably London, Wales, Norway and Switzerland. It was probably Henry James' military career that had led to his love of travel. He served as a midshipman in HMS *Blenheim* during the Baltic Campaign of 1855, and was commissioned as a lieutenant into the Royal Gloucestershire Regiment of Hussar Yeomanry in 1865. When he was home Henry James' passion for hunting took priority over estate matters and on many occasions he wrote to his agent of his need to borrow money to cover

The Lodge. *WHH. Clifford.*   August 8th 1885.

his outgoings: 'Can you think how to raise £400 for me? When I return home next week I will literally not have a penny until next rent day.'

The third of Edmund's difficulties related to the managing of the estate. Cottage tenants had become used to the benevolence of Henry Clifford Clifford who, in many instances, had not reviewed their rents for at least thirty years. The farmers' rents had been looked at on a more regular basis, but even so were probably in need of review. Henry James therefore desired that the estate be revalued in 1867, and rents charged accordingly. Some of the tenant farmers complained of the poor state of their buildings and it is likely that several of the cottages were in need of repair too, all at the expense of Henry James Clifford who was reluctant to spend any of his money on maintenance unless it was essential. All types of excuses were used, particularly by the farmers, to delay paying their rents, some being looked upon more favourably than others. The farmer whose crops were destroyed by rabbits was given a second chance, whilst the agent was instructed to deal with one particularly troublesome farmer: 'Please get his rent as soon as you can and if he humbugs take proceeding against him.'

Despite his deficiencies, Henry James did maintain an interest in the running of the estate, and on one occasion chastised his agent for settling bills on his behalf and recording a rent incorrectly: 'I prefer to settle my bills myself. I see you have put me down as having received £25 from William Turner, whereas I have only received £20 19s. 17d.'

One of Henry James' first public acts following the death of his grandfather was the giving of some land to permit the enlargement of the churchyard, and six months later he let 10 acres of land to members of the Mechanics' Institute for use as allotments. (This was not without its problems, as several people tried to join the Institute for the sole purpose of obtaining an allotment thereby prompting the vicar to say: 'Perhaps some of those who come to dig may stay to read.') Henry James was one of the two managers of the Penny Bank when it opened in 1864 (the other was the vicar) and was also president of the Mechanics' Institute on a number of occasions. A supporter of all local charities, he helped to relieve the poor during the winter by giving coals at Christmas and contributing towards the annual soup kitchen.

After several daughters, the birth of his son, Henry Francis, in 1871 was the cause of much celebration and all the village children were given the afternoon off school to attend a party at Frampton Court.

Frampton Lodge

The original part of Frampton Lodge, consisting of the four right-hand bays, was built in the late 17th or early 18th century. The property was enlarged in the late 18th or early 19th century and the main door was moved to a central position. It is possible that the original building was only two storeys in height.

Marianne Clifford

Captioned Mrs. H. Clifford, this sketch refers to Marianne Clifford (1816-88) the widow of Henry John Clifford (1810-52). Marianne and Henry John, the parents of Henry James Clifford (above), had probably started living in Frampton Lodge following their marriage in 1838.

Widowed at the age of 36, Marianne brought up her six surviving children (two had died in infancy) with the help of a governess, two nurserymaids, a cook, a footman, and a housemaid. The staff were reduced to three once the children had grown up. Each year Marianne Clifford contributed £10 towards the running of the National School and £2 to the little Dame School at Fromebridge.

From September 1861 it appears that Marianne Clifford and her family left Frampton for a while:

FRAMPTON LODGE

TO BE LET, furnished, from Michaelmas next, for six, nine, or twelve months, comprising dining and drawing-room, library, schoolroom, 4 best bedrooms, dressing-room, 4 secondary bedrooms, 2 servants' rooms, and offices, with good Stabling, Garden, and Orchard.

The above Residence is situated in the pleasant village of Frampton, about 3½ miles from the Stonehouse Station on the Midland Railway, and in a good hunting neighbourhood.

Apply to Henry Bruton, Estate and House Agent, King Street, Gloucester.

Gloucester Journal, 24 August 1861

8 FITCHERBURY – 7 October 1865

Job Browning

Job Browning (*c.*1816-87) was an agricultural carter who came to live at what was then, rather grandly, called Fisherbury Castle sometime between 1851 and 1861. He was born in Tetbury, the family having moved to Frampton during his childhood. His father, Henry Browning, was a gamekeeper and probably worked for the Clifford family estate.

Job and his wife Sarah had seven children. He was illiterate and although Job described his daughters as 'scholars' on the census returns they were far from regular attenders of the National School. The family must have been among the poorest of the village for a benefactor paid their weekly school fees, and yet the logbook is littered with entries such as: 'Oct. 12th 1864 – J. and S. Browning, after coming irregularly for a few weeks, are away again. For how long it is utterly impossible to guess – the mischief of being paid for.'

Thomas Draper

Thomas Draper (*c.*1829-96) was living in the other half of the property in 1851 with his wife Ann whom he had married two years earlier. He was born in Frampton and she in the neighbouring village of Eastington. After a short time at another property in Frampton they returned to Fitcherbury but, suffering with rheumatism, Thomas was by 1871 unable to work. As an agricultural labourer he would have endured long hours toiling on the land in all winds and weathers and it was probably this that led him to spend the latter part of his life as a rheumatic cripple.

R. Allen. The Shepherd's Cottage

9 THE SHEPHERD'S COTTAGE (NOW KEEPER'S COTTAGE) – undated

Robert Allen

Known as Park Cottage in 1851 and Park in 1861, this property was occupied by Robert Allen, a shepherd. He was born in Tetbury *c.*1823. His wife Maria came either from Ampney Crucis or Prestbury (the censuses differ). Robert Allen was unable to write, but his only child, Jane, attended the National School. Robert's cucumbers won the best brace competition at the Frampton and Fretherne Cottage Gardeners' Society show in 1863.

10 ALFRED DRAPER'S COTTAGE FROM THE PLANTATION BY THE SHEPHERDS – 30 May 1867

This cottage was located at the westerly edge of Townfield.

Alfred Draper

Alfred Draper, a labourer born in Frampton *c.*1831, was a younger brother of Thomas (see sketch 8). Before coming to this cottage he had lived with his father first at Fitcherbury and then Greycroft (on the western side of The Street). By 1871 he had moved in with his sister Charlotte Wilks in her cottage on The Green. Alfred appears to have died at the Wheatenhurst Union Workhouse in 1898.

a. Draper's Cottage from the
may 30th 1867 Plantation by the Shepherd's.

11 THE GREEN (EAST) SOUTH OF FRAMPTON COURT – 9 August 1865

The Old Coffee House

William Turner

This had been the Turner family home since before 1835, and when his parents, Thomas and Sarah, moved to Denfurlong Farm, William, his wife Ann and their children continued to live there. William Turner was born *c*.1824 in Frampton. A butcher by trade, he had a 16-year-old apprentice and a housemaid living in according to the 1861 census. In 1863 William Turner appeared before the magistrates on a charge of selling unwholesome beef that had not been correctly slaughtered. Evidence was heard from Thomas Turner to the effect that he had fed his son's cow in the morning but on return from church in the afternoon William found the cow to be dying. The cowman was of the opinion that it had been given too much corn. Several local farmers from Frampton confirmed that the beast had been fit and healthy. The meat inspector advised that the beast had not been properly killed and that, whilst the meat did not look very good, it was fit for human consumption. The case against William Turner was dismissed. William is last mentioned in Frampton in *Slater's Directory* of 1868 and by 1871 the cottage was occupied by George Hobbs, another butcher, and his family.

Early in 1877, with the property empty, the vicar put forward the idea that it be turned into a coffee house with a bright warm reading room for winter evenings and snug benches and tables in the garden in the summer under the shade of the fine sycamore tree. He thought of the name 'Tree Coffee House' and proposed that it sell coffee, tea, cocoa and other harmless drinks at 1d. per cup with eatables at modest charges. Writing paper, envelopes and the use of a pen were to be available at the cost of ½d. Pipes would be allowed and the idea of a skittle

Stable doors. August 9 1/65. *William Turner's.*

alley was discussed, but there was to be no gambling or alcoholic drink. The vicar also promised 'no attempts at thrusting religious instruction'.

Four hundred shares were issued at 2s. 6d. each to raise the necessary funds for furniture etc., with the possession of a share constituting membership. Nearly eighty locals attended the opening on 28 June 1877. Two weeks later the vicar announced his intention to establish the Frampton Branch of the Church of England Temperance Society and with support from the minister of the Congregational Chapel, the Rev. W. Lewis, he secured the services of several speakers so that by the spring of 1878 there were 70 total abstainers in the village. One particularly powerful orator explained that £150 million was wasted annually in England on drink – which put in simple terms meant the equivalent of placing 30 sovereigns on each letter of the Bible.

Albert Fryer, a watchmaker from Arlingham, and his family took over the running of The Coffee House late in 1878. As a total abstainer he set an excellent example and by the end of 1880 membership increased to well over 100. A meeting in a local warehouse in October of that year attracted between 300 and 400 people from Frampton and neighbouring parishes.

Manor Cottage

Henry Hulbert

The caption 'George' Hulbert is a mystery for the census returns and other written sources suggest that Henry Hulbert and his family were living in this house from before 1851 until *c.*1867 after which he bought a house and land in The Street. (Perhaps 'George' was a nickname

George Hulbert.   *Charles Hobbs*   *Pick. Russell.*

or a rare error in the titling.) Henry (*c*.1816-82) was a tailor from Winterbourne and counted Henry Clifford Clifford amongst his customers, making, altering and repairing many types of garments including dressing gowns, trousers, coats and waistcoats. He also made clothes for the servants; a suit of stable clothes being £2 10s., the same price as a suit of clothes for a page. The normal practice in Frampton for any tradesman carrying out work for the Clifford family was to receive settlement of his bills twice yearly at the time his own rent was due. Henry married twice, firstly to Harriet and then to Elizabeth.

Charles Hobbs

The cottage in which Charles Hobbs and his family lived burnt down c.1950.

Charles Hobbs was a captain and barge owner born in Frampton *c*.1807. His first wife, Patience, came from Cheltenham and although the Hobbs had at least eight children only the two youngest were living at home by the time they moved to the cottage shown.

During the 1860s Charles owned several vessels all of which appear to have operated along the Gloucester and Berkeley Canal, River Severn and Bristol Channel. At least two of Charles' sons followed their father to sea, Gabriel being master of his father's vessel *Palace* for some time.

It appears that towards the end of the 1860s Charles retired from sailing but he still maintained his business, and at his death in 1884 he left his two trows to his second wife, Sarah Ann. Trows were sailing barges once common on the River Severn and its navigable tributaries where they were the main form of transport for goods over many centuries. The trow's trough-like shape was designed to meet the characteristics of the Severn, a particularly hazardous river

FRETHERNE BRIDGE, GLOUCESTER AND
BERKELEY CANAL
TO BE SOLD BY AUCTION,
By JAMES KARN,
At the WHARF, near the above Bridge, on Thursday, the
18th day of March, 1869, precisely at three o'clock,—

THE TROW, "PALACE," (Burthen 85 Tons),
together with all her standing and running Rigging,
Boat, Oars, &c. &c.
She is a fast sailing Vessel, and well adapted for the
Bridgewater Trade, in which she has been employed until
a short time ago.
For a list of Stores, and to view, apply to Mr. John
Burr, Frampton-on-Severn.

Gloucester Journal, 13 March 1869

with its tidal range of between forty and fifty feet, the second largest in the world. The flat-bottomed boats were developed to go over the ever-shifting sandbanks and cope with the fast-flowing tide. On board the master and crew would sleep in cabins under the decked sections of the bow and stern. The open hold enabled cargo to be heaped very high. Where a trow was not able to sail, for instance on the Gloucester and Berkeley Canal, it was towed by donkeys or horses.

White House

Joseph Pick

Joseph Pick (*c.*1816-93) was a sawyer who, in later life, became a coal merchant and baker. He earned 3s. a day as a sawyer when making a wicket gate for Thomas Karn at the *Bell Inn* in 1871. Joseph was born in North Nibley, as were his wife Elizabeth and their older children, and he brought the family to this cottage in Frampton just prior to 1851.

Their children all went to school, with one of their sons, Daniel, becoming a pupil teacher at Framilode British School where he served his apprenticeship until 1861 when he reached the age of 18. By the time of his marriage three years later, Daniel was a schoolmaster. A daughter, Fanny, later had a grocer's and draper's shop in what is now called Cardiff House, next to the Heart of Oak in The Street (west) where in 1891 the widowed Joseph was living with her. Another child, William, was an ostler at the *Bell Inn* and lived at the top of The Green in the 1860s and early 1870s.

Russell

The tenant of this cottage which, like others situated nearby belonged to Henry Clifford Clifford, was probably James Russell who spent a short while in the village during the mid-1860s.

Parks Cottage

The original part of Parks Cottage lies to the north (left) and probably dates to the early 17th century. The property was enlarged in the late 18th or early 19th century. Over the years the cottage has been home to labourers working on Parks Farm.

Thomas Lodge

Thomas Lodge, born in Frampton *c.*1809, was the captain of a vessel and as a mariner would have spent weeks away from home, leaving Mary his wife to bring up the family. They had married just after the census was taken in 1841 and moved to the northerly half of Parks Cottage.

During the early part of 1864 Julia Lodge, Thomas' 15-year-old daughter, was a popular performer at concerts in the village, singing such pieces as *Sing, Birdie, Sing*. One concert, in February of that year, was held to raise funds for the Gloucester Infirmary.

The Lodge family occupied Parks Cottage probably until the deaths of Mary and Thomas within three months of each other in 1900.

Miriam Harmer

Samuel Harmer, a cabinet maker, had died aged 70 in 1851 leaving Miriam a widow. She was a charwoman and times were hard for, having been born *c.*1790, she could not have found employment easy at her advanced age.

One son, John, followed his father's trade of cabinet maker. He married and his wife Hannah bore him several children. When she died in 1864 at the age of 48, he was left with his two youngest children to care for and he appears to have found this a difficult task. Two years later he was up before the magistrates at the tiny court room above the *Whitminster Inn*, Whitminster for deserting his children.

A simple entry in the National School's logbook records the same event: 'Little Harmer gone to the Union. It has long been threatened and now it is done'.

By the time of the 1871 census Miriam, at the age of 81, was too old to work and John and his youngest daughter were living with her. Both Miriam and John spent their final days at the Wheatenhurst Union, dying in 1874 and 1887 respectively.

WHITMINSTER PETTY SESSIONS, THURSDAY.— (Before H. H. Wilton, W. Davies, and J. Grey, Esqrs. and the Rev. Thomas Peters.)—DESERTING CHILDREN.—*John Harmer*, a carpenter, of Frampton-on-Severn, was charged with leaving his two children chargeable to the Wheatenhurst Union.

Mr. Cother, Governor of the Union, deposed that the prisoner's two children were in the Union, chargeable to the Parish. He had left the children with his mother, and refused to maintain them. His wages were 14*s*. a-week, and he was stopping at a beershop, and spending his money. Sentenced to fourteen days' imprisonment.

Gloucester Journal, 16 June 1866

Nastfield Cottage

Nastfield Cottage was probably built during the early or mid-17th century. Traditionally the home of workers at Nastfield Farm, Henry Haines, John Hale and George Bird may well have been employed there.

Thomas Lodge.   Miriam Harmer.   Henry Haines.   (J.) Hale George Bird.

Henry Haines

Henry Haines was a labourer, born in Frampton *c.*1808. He had come to the northerly part of Nastfield Cottage sometime between 1841 and 1851. His wife Hannah had previously been married to Charles Niblett, a carpenter, with whom she had had several children. After Henry's death in 1869 Hannah probably remained at the cottage until she died in 1885.

John Hale and George Bird

John Hale and George Bird shared the other half of Nastfield Cottage and were both agricultural labourers. They may have been related, although no indication of this is given in the various census returns.

John Hale was born in Tortworth, although the exact year of his birth is not known. His age varies on each of the censuses; he could have been born as early as 1773 or as late as 1778 according to the information given. When he died in 1878 the entry in the parish magazine gave his age as 92, but this was corrected two months later with an apology which stated that although he believed himself to be over 100 years of age the entry should have read 99 as nobody had ever been able to trace any precise details regarding his birth. (This highlights the problems for the illiterate who were often unable to give the correct information about themselves.)

It is likely that John Hale had come to Frampton in 1810 as a labourer from Tortworth, with his wife Mary and their three-week-old daughter. According to the Parish Overseers' papers his age was given as 24 which would have made his birth-date *c.*1786.

George Bird and his wife Elizabeth Ann were married in 1858 and may have moved to the cottage at that time. George originated from Tetbury and was born *c.*1832. They had four

c. Wilks.   James Smith a Burg.   August /65.

surviving sons, one of their boys appearing to have died in infancy. Elizabeth Bird was a nurse and may have helped John Hale through the latter years of his life.

Charlotte Wilks

George Stratford, Frampton's thatcher, previously occupied the cottage shown. He had died in 1842 and from that day onwards there was no resident thatcher in the village, despite there being so many thatched buildings. During the 1860s it is likely that members of the Gardner family living in the nearby villages of Moreton Valence and Longney carried out thatching in Frampton on Severn. (There is evidence that they completed work in the village in the early 1870s.)

John Wilks, Charlotte's husband, was a greengrocer from Wotton-under-Edge, and in 1851 John, his mother Mary Gabb and a lodger called Charles Bennett lived in the property. The small building adjoining the cottage may have been the greengrocer's shop.

John's untimely death at the age of 33 left his wife Charlotte to bring up four children under the age of six and these attended both the Chapel and National Schools. John's mother remained with the family working first as a staymaker (stays were corsets with bones in them) and then as a sempstress (seamstress). To make ends meet Charlotte (c.1822-97) was a laundress, one of many in the village. (In those days it was not always

FRAMPTON-ON-SEVERN.

Fatal Accident.—On Tuesday a man named John Wilkes, hallier, and dealer of Frampton, was conveying with his horse and cart, a load of goods from Frocester station to Frampton, and when near Frocester he fell from the load upon which he was riding, and fractured his skull. He was picked up alive, but whilst being conveyed to the George at Frocester he expired. He has left a wife and five children.

Gloucester Chronicle, 4 February 1860

August 24ᵗʰ/85.   *Miss Werrett.*

possible for even the poorer families to do all their own washing because people had neither the facilities nor the equipment to manage the weekly wash.)

The Firs

These two adjoining houses were built during the middle to late 18th century.

James Smith

James Smith (*c*.1812–81) followed in his father Charles' footsteps as the village's cooper, and as such would have served a seven-year apprenticeship, for coopering was a highly specialised craft. Since pre-biblical times commodities were shipped or moved in barrels because of their exceptional strength and their wheel-like qualities which facilitated easy movement in the days when power was dependent upon the muscles of man or beast. In addition to wine, spirits and beer, barrels were used for the storage of flour, barley, sugar, potatoes, fruit and many other kinds of goods. Even gunpowder was kept in extra strong casks made specially for the task. The work of the cooper was not restricted to barrelmaking, as buckets for water and milking, bowls for washing, dolly tubs for laundering and jugs were all made by him. Many of these would have lasted a lifetime and become valued possessions among the folk in Frampton. Even chairs made from cut-away barrels would have been popular in the poorer homes.

James Smith often made coopered goods for Frampton Court and repaired items when necessary. These included corks, bungs, sieves, buckets, casks, work tubs, the hooping of chimney pots and making of besoms. Henry Clifford Clifford settled James Smith's bill twice a year, on 1 January and 1 July, when the annual rental on his house, workshops and orchard of £15 1s. 0d. was due. The Firs had been James' home for many years, his father having also

Mrs Watts.

run his business from the property.

James Smith married Ellen, a girl from Shapwick in Somerset, in the mid-1850s and they had four children. After James' death Ellen became an Inland Revenue Tax Collector.

Ann King

The widow of Daniel King, a shoemaker, Ann was born in Frampton *c.*1812. They were together for three short years before Daniel died aged 30. Their only surviving daughter, Frances Mary, was baptised two weeks after his death.

Surrounded by her family, Ann King made the best of her life and immediately threw herself into her work. She was a straw hat maker, teaching the trade to her niece who was apprenticed to her. The hats were made from straw plait and it was possible to make 40 yards of plait in a day lasting 12 hours. The plait was sewn into the desired shape of a hat or bonnet, then stiffened by being pressed through a solution of gelatin and dried, before being shaped in a press.

Ann's mother, Nancy Bennett (who had run the post office for many years), and later her brother John and sister Mary, lived with her. They did not stay very long in The Firs, moving to Cardiff House in The Street (west) where Ann probably remained until her death in 1885.

13   THE GREEN (EAST) – 24 August 1865

Hadley's Farm

The name Hadley's Farm is given in various trade directories of the period and presumably included a nearby field which was known as Hadley's Piece.

Ann and Mary Amelia Wherrett

Ann (c.1806-86) and Mary Amelia Wherrett (c.1820-98) were sisters who took over the running of Hadley's Farm from their mother (also Mary) who had died in 1859, their father Thomas having died in 1847.

Ann and Mary's brother, Charles, also lived with them, assisting on the farm which comprised 75 acres. Milk, butter, eggs, potatoes and hay were among the commodities produced on the farm where pigs were also kept. Three-and-a-half quarts of milk cost 10½d. Most items required on the farm were either made or purchased locally and this is illustrated by the purchase of a stepladder for 10s. from John Millard, a sawyer who lived in Frampton. The sisters later moved to Oegrove Farm further down the village.

Farmers such as the Wherretts would have traded at the annual Frampton Fat Cattle Fair which was held on the third Tuesday in February:

> FAIR.—On Tuesday, the 16th inst., the fair was held on the Green. The stock on offer comprised about 50 sheep, between 20 and 30 pigs, and three or four beasts. Mutton fetched from 7½d. to 8d. per lb., and pigs realised very high prices. There was a very fair trade, and good articles fetched corresponding prices.

Gloucester Chronicle, 20 February 1869

The Grange

A large detached house, The Grange was built early in the 17th century. It was refronted in the early 18th century and altered and enlarged during the 19th century.

Ann Watts

Ann Watts was the widow of Thomas Watts, surgeon, who had died in 1855. He had been held in such high esteem that a Memorial Fund was immediately founded with even the very poorest villagers donating a penny or two. Ann Watts had been born c.1789 in Doynton, south Gloucestershire, and living with her in 1861 were her two spinster daughters Elizabeth and Anne, a cook, housemaid and groom.

The Watts were a charitable family doing much for the poor of the village. In 1837 Ann Watts established a Female Septennial Benefit Club 'for the purpose of rendering pecuniary and medical relief to its members in (times of) sickness'. Ann successfully ran the club until the end of its first seven-year term, whereupon she relinquished her position because of failing health. (The person in the bathchair in the foreground of the sketch is probably Ann Watts.) The immense success of the female club gave rise to the establishment of a Male Septennial Benefit Club in 1844, and the two organisations were then run by her daughter Anne and son Thomas, who acted as treasurers. Thomas, who like his father was the local surgeon, was a busy man and most of the work of the Clubs was left to Anne. Held high in the affection of the villagers, Anne was presented with an illuminated vellum address on the occasion of the 35th and 28th anniversaries of the two Clubs, in which mention is made of the way she had detected and punished impostors, genuinely applied relief where it was needed and managed

Oct. 7th H. Greening. Thomas Hunt. E. Clarke. Brazington.

the finances of £9,690 between Sickness (£3,316), Funerals (£1,323) and Septennial Divisions (£5,051). Organisation of the Septennial meetings was no small task, with 450 people sitting down to a meal in a marquee at the back of the Watts' house.

The Watts family were also regular contributors towards the general running of the National School where Anne frequently visited to inspect the needlework and take the children to church practice. Each year she awarded the two best attenders of each class with a prize, and it was not unknown for her quietly to pay the fees of some of the poorer children to enable them to remain at school. Mindful of those less fortunate than themselves, the Watts gave generously to all village charities such as a soup kitchen and coals for the poor, and Anne also ran a clothing club.

The Watts ladies moved to the house now known as Top O' the Green *c*.1877. Ann Watts died in 1883 and her daughter Anne in 1906.

14   ADVOWSONS – 7 October 1865

This cottage was located very close to the old tithe barn at the end of Watery Lane which is now used by Frampton Sailing Club. Its name suggests that it originally formed part of Advowson Farm and had possibly been home to some of the farm labourers.

Hannah Greening, Thomas Hunt, Eliza Clarke and William Brazington

The first three names mentioned on the sketch comprised one household of which Thomas Hunt (*c*.1791-1868) was the head. A widower, he was employed as an agricultural labourer. His daughter Eliza had married another agricultural labourer, Benjamin Clarke from Eastington, in 1855. (It is not clear why the caption favours Eliza rather than her husband.) Also in their

family was Henry Trueman, Thomas Hunt's grandson. Henry's mother had died in childbirth and his young father, a labourer from Wednesbury, must have decided to let the boy be brought up in Frampton by his aunt and grandfather.

Hannah Greening (born *c*.1782 in Frampton) had been a lodger of Thomas Hunt's on the 1861 census, but she appears to have died in November 1862. There were at least two Hannah Greenings in Frampton during the 19th century and some confusion may have arisen, particularly as Hannah Greening's name seems to have been added to the caption.

William Brazington (or Brazenton) was born in Ashleworth *c*.1804. His accent caused the enumerators of the censuses problems as this was variously written Ashlechurch and Aishlaw. He married Mary Bird in 1827 when neither could write their names. The couple had several children all of which had left home by the time the sketch was drawn.

15 BOTTOM OF THE GREEN – 8 October 1865

Advowson Farm

This property is one of the oldest in the village, dating back to the late 15th century. Originally it was constructed as an open hall of three bays, a service area of two bays, the final bay being a solar. Floors were inserted in the 17th century and the house underwent further alterations in the 1700s. In about 1830 the owner reputedly obtained the present windows from a church and fitted them into his property.

Richard Stiff

At the time of the sketches Richard Stiff (*c*.1822-78) was probably running Advowson Farm following the death of his father Nehemiah in 1864. He was also continuing with his bakery

business on the other side of The Green at Sunny Side, and as a consequence of this his name appears under both properties on the drawings. Elizabeth Stiff, Nehemiah's widow was actively involved with the farm, which later passed to her daughter Mary Ann. This was not unusual, for women often carried on the farming business when their husbands or fathers died.

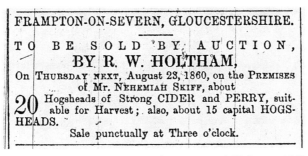

FRAMPTON-ON-SEVERN, GLOUCESTERSHIRE.

TO BE SOLD BY AUCTION,
BY R. W. HOLTHAM,
On THURSDAY NEXT, August 23, 1860, on the PREMISES
of Mr. NEHEMIAH SKIFF, about
20 Hogsheads of Strong CIDER and PERRY, suitable for Harvest; also, about 15 capital HOGSHEADS.
Sale punctually at Three o'clock.

Gloucester Journal, 18 August 1860

Tom Clarke's Cottage
Built in the late 16th or early 17th century, by the time of the sketch this cottage probably consisted of a sitting room, kitchen, back kitchen (with pump, soft water tank and bread oven) and three bedrooms.

John Goatman

John Goatman (*c*.1823-72) was an agricultural implement/machine maker who, during the 1860s, lived in this cottage with his wife Ann, son John George and brother Thomas (another agricultural implement/machine maker). He also made and supplied gates and all the associated fixings such as latches, hinges, screws and nails. John Goatman owned the cottage, which, when he died rather suddenly from apoplexy aged only 49, passed in ownership to his son, John George. He was known as the tallest and strongest man in Frampton, and wore spectacles to read. John Goatman was one of the leading figures in the campaign to have Whitminster Lane, a private road which was frequently too poorly maintained to use, transferred into public ownership.

Site of Prospect Cottage

The cottage has since been demolished and Prospect Cottage built as a matching pair for Fernleigh.

Kitty Wilkins

Known variously as Catherine, Christiana or Kitty Wilkins, she was the wife of James, a butcher, who died late in 1865. As her name is shown on the sketch it seems likely that James was being looked after in the sick ward at the Wheatenhurst Union Workhouse. Kitty (c.1784-1879) came from Stanley in Gloucestershire (either Kings Stanley or Leonard Stanley). She was for many years a recipient of money from the Wicks Charity which had been set up following the death of Ann Wicks, daughter of a former vicar of the parish, to provide a small legacy for Frampton's aged poor.

Gloucester Journal, 6 June 1868

Fernleigh

William Coole

William, the son of Peter Coole (of *The Three Horseshoes*), was a blacksmith and there is evidence that, like other farriers, he acted as the village's veterinary surgeon. He was involved in sporting activities in the village as the newspaper extract opposite shows.

William (c.1836-87) was born in Frampton and married Laura Hawkins Ballinger in Gloucester in 1861. It was probably at this time that they moved to Fernleigh. By 1871 he and his wife Laura had four children, a servant and an apprentice living with them.

William would have learned his trade from his father Peter. The blacksmith's part in the daily needs of village life was

Gloucester Journal, 28 September 1867

fundamental and his skills would have included farriery in addition to the repair of tools and equipment. He would also have assisted other craftsmen such as wheelwrights by putting the iron tyres around their wheels. The hours were long and hard and the Cooles may well have worked from 6a.m. until 6p.m. whenever daylight permitted.

In about 1872, following his father's remarriage and retirement, William returned to live at *The Three Horseshoes*.

Cottages on the site of The Trillium, The Street (west)

William Clarke

William Clarke and his wife Mary lived in several different houses in Frampton, moving to the one immediately behind John Ballinger's bakery sometime during the early 1860s. He was an agricultural labourer/gardener who had been born in Frampton *c*.1815.

John Tilley Ford

John Tilley Ford (*c*.1819–1910) was a boot and shoemaker from Uley who, with his wife Mary, had at least thirteen children which seemed to attend both the Chapel and National Schools. John and Mary's grave in the churchyard at St Mary's lies among so many others belonging to people featured in these sketches.

In 1856, at the end of the Crimean War, the Singer sewing machine was introduced from America and modified to stitch leather, thereby marking a turning point in the manufacture of shoes and boots. Before the end of the 1850s several shoemaking factories had been built and the mechanisation of the shoe industry developed over the next thirty years. The effects of this progress were gradually felt in Frampton during the 1860s, its six shoemakers in 1861 reduced to three by 1871. Nevertheless John Tilley Ford passed his craft to two of his sons, perhaps hoping that the days of a village shoemaker were to remain. It is likely that other members of his family were involved in the making of shoes; traditionally women were employed to bind shoes and sew the quarters together.

Paper on the Merits of Pure and Cross-bred Sheep.

FRAMPTON-ON-SEVERN. — STEEPLE-CHASES. This sporting affair, which had for the past week caused so much excitement in this and the neighbouring villages, came off on Thursday, the 12th inst., the place of starting being fixed near the walk locks on the Stroud Canal, and the course being across the meadows to the banks of the river Froome, from thence back by a different course to the place of starting. The course was interspersed with numerous leaps, many being by no means of an easy description; the distance of the course may be estimated at 2½ miles. Three started, but one refusing the first leap, the trial lay between the other two. This race was won by Henry Clifford, Esq., jun., with his favourite mare Beeswing, though closely followed by his younger brother, Walter Clifford, Esq., upon the celebrated old hunter Charlie, which made excellent work. The course was then run a second time by the same two horses, the third refusing the first leap as before. This race was a repetition of the former. Some foot races then took place and were eagerly contested, and some first-rate running and brook leaping were displayed. The next part of the programme consisted of a flat race, which was contested by four horses, and was won after a hard struggle by Mr. Wm. Coole, of Frampton, upon his beautiful chestnut pony Professor. In the second heat Mr. Coole won as before. The company, which was numerous, now dispersed much delighted with the novel scene, thankful for the treat the gentlemen had afforded, and trusting at the proper time to be gratified with a repetition. We believe the stakes were merely nominal.

Gloucester Chronicle, 21 April 1860

Edward Evans

Born *c*.1821 in Frampton, Edward Evans was the son of William Evans, a stone mason. Edward did not follow his father's trade; instead he chose to become a waterman, perhaps wishing to explore the world outside the village. To the evident frustration of the schoolmaster, Edward and Ann Evans' five children did not receive a full education by any means: 'Sept. 6th 1865 – Flora Evans, who attended two and a half days last week, has not been here since Monday morning: the three days I suppose will have to suffice for the next twelve months.'

Leather Bottle Lane

William Hyett

Leather Bottle Lane was situated between the cottage of Edward Evans and the shop of Caroline Ward and is now known as Wards Court. (On the 1841 census it appeared as Rag Mop Alley.) Although only the cottage of William Hyett (*c.*1815-71) is shown on this sketch, the lane is nevertheless worthy of mention for it was the scene of the most brutal event in Frampton during the 1860s and possibly throughout the entire 19th century. The tale is told using extracts from the *Gloucester Journal, Gloucester Chronicle*, Frampton Parish Magazine and the Gloucester Gaol records.

On Friday 5 September 1862 around lunchtime, a quarrel developed between two elderly occupants of cottages in Leather Bottle Lane: Elizabeth Webb aged 80 and Mary Humberstone, 60. The two women had argued before and on this particular occasion they stood at their respective doors and had a heated exchange of words. Mary Humberstone was incensed and told her friend Caroline Grey, 'That old woman has been talking about me, and telling lies,' but Caroline Grey replied, 'I don't believe it; she is such a quiet woman.' Undeterred, Humberstone went into her cottage to fetch a fire shovel.

When she emerged, a passing neighbour, David Dunn, on seeing the shovel in Humberstone's hand, tried to prevent the matter going any further, but such was the passion of the disagreement between the women that Humberstone dealt Elizabeth Webb a blow over the right eye, which immediately bled. The older woman wiped her eye with her apron and walked back into her house where she lived with her daughter and son-in-law, Sarah and William Hyett. Her daughter put a plaster over the wound and sent for the doctor, Thomas Watts. He found the wound to be very superficial and reportedly thought nothing of it. Elizabeth Webb died later during the night and Mary Humberstone was taken into custody six days later charged with manslaughter.

The villagers spoke of murder and Frampton was in a state of excitement as the events unfolded. A native of Carmarthen, Mary Humberstone was the wife of a hawker, George. The couple had been in the village for about ten years and had previously lived in Whitminster Lane. She was almost five feet tall with dark grey hair and grey eyes. Blind in her left eye, she had a large nose and had lost most of her teeth.

The inquest on Elizabeth Webb, the widow of a shoemaker, was held at the *Bell Inn* and Mr. Watts' postmortem was later to provide the vital evidence which acquitted Humberstone of the charge of manslaughter. The doctor felt that the blow to the head neither caused nor accelerated the death, but that it was the condition of the muscular tissues of the heart, brought on by the excitement and passion of the argument, that was eventually to prove fatal.

At her subsequent appearance at the Quarter Sessions a month later, Mary Humberstone was sentenced to six weeks imprisonment for wounding Elizabeth Webb, a particularly lenient punishment given the circumstances.

In 1869 Leather Bottle Lane was the location of another bizarre incident which, fortunately, had a happier ending.

ATTEMPTED SUICIDE. — *George Charles*, a labourer of Frampton, was charged with attempting to commit suicide by hanging himself in his bedroom.—Peter Coole, a blacksmith of Frampton, said: About seven o'clock on the night of the 31st ult. I went to the prisoner's house, hearing groans I burst the front door, went up stairs, and found him hanging by the neck. I cut the cord, unfastened it from his neck, and placed him on the bed. I thought he was dead; it was some time before I saw any sign of life in him.—The prisoner's wife, who was present, said he was subject to fits when he drank. That day he had drunk a quantity of cider.—Prisoner said: I am a discharged soldier. When in India I had a sun stroke. When I drink any beer or spirits my head is affected, and I don't know what I am doing. I have now signed the pledge and will never drink any more liquor.—The Bench: You must abstain in future from drinking. It was a mercy your life had not been sacrificed. You are now discharged.

Gloucester Journal, 10 April 1869

16   ROAD LEADING TO THE CHURCH (THE STREET) – 26 August 1865

Tamaris Cottage

This small detached cottage was probably built during the 16th century.

William Gould

William Gould was a marine store dealer born in Worcestershire *c.*1808. With his wife Jane (who came from Dursley), he lived in this cottage throughout the 1860s.

It is likely that William and Jane witnessed the unusual occurrence of an earthquake on Tuesday 6 October 1863. At about 3.20a.m. most of the villagers were awakened by an extraordinarily loud report, and many felt the shock very distinctly, as if it were an upheaving of their beds. Jugs and basins were heard to rattle and bells to ring, and one person in the neighbourhood who had fixed an alarm bell to each window shutter, is said to have mistaken the earthquake for a band of robbers.

The earthquake was felt throughout the southern and western parts of England, lasted for between 6 and 12 seconds and was well documented in the newspapers of the day. Several theories were advanced regarding the cause. Some thought that the gases inside the earth bubbled up and exploded, whilst others felt the movement was horizontal, following the course of certain rocks or strata. Another theory was that the motion was circular or gyratory, as if two currents were moving round in opposite directions and often coming into contact with one another.

On the evening of 30 October 1868 another earthquake was felt in the village and surrounding area.

Marda House

Hobbs (see sketch 52; these two families may have been identified the wrong way around)

There were several Hobbs families in Frampton during the 1860s. The most likely family to have lived in the house depicted was that of George and Emma Hobbs who married in 1857.

George was the son of Charles Hobbs, a barge owner who lived on The Green (east). He had followed his father to sea. Emma's maiden name was also Hobbs although their two families were not closely related. George appears to have got himself into trouble at the Frampton Feast in 1860.

> George Hobbs, waterman, of Frampton, was charged with assaulting Eliza Cooke, at Frampton, on the 20th inst. The defendant jumped upon complainant's back at Frampton feast, which she complained of, when he attempted to kick her. He was fined 1s. and costs.

Gloucester Chronicle, 15 September 186

Ad Extremum

Joseph Dowdeswell Orchard

Joseph Dowdeswell Orchard was born *c.*1830 in Frocester. He was a tallow chandler and married Esther, the daughter of another tallow chandler (Joseph Watkins) in 1852.

The villagers of Frampton would have relied upon tallow candles to light their homes. Tallow, which is animal fat separated from the membranous matter which might putrefy, comes mainly from bullocks and sheep. Generally the cheaper candles would have been made from beef tallow, whilst better quality ones contained both beef and mutton tallow in roughly equal proportions.

The first stage of candlemaking was rendering the tallow, a laborious and rather smelly process done in a large cauldron or boiler made of iron or copper. The waste materials rose to the surface, with any remaining impurities being separated by the addition of water, causing them to settle in a layer between the water and fat. The tallow was then strained and kept in storage tubs.

The wicks for tallow candles comprised several strands of pure cotton that was bought in large balls or skeins. As the strands were cut a slight twist was added so that the candles would burn without undue spluttering. The wicks were then arranged on special rods called broaches and dipped into a vessel of molten tallow. After the tallow had hardened they were dipped repeatedly until the candles reached the required thickness.

Advances in candlemaking in the 19th century gradually saw the demise of the tallow chandler and by 1857 the first paraffin wax candles appeared on the market. Brighter, cleaner and more regular in form, they were manufactured wholesale and cheaply. By the 1860s paraffin lamps were also widely available.

It is not surprising then, to find Joseph Dowdeswell Orchard changing his occupation during the 1860s from tallow chandler to carrier. A later advertisement in *Kelly's Directory* of 1889 shows him carrying to Gloucester on Wednesdays and Saturdays, returning the same day.

Joseph and Esther had 10 children including Inkerman (born 1856) who was named after the scene of a battle in south Crimea in 1854. Following Esther's death Joseph married twice more, to Sarah Agnes Bennett and then Sarah Ann Hobbs. He died in 1922.

Charles Neale (see sketch 17); John Ballinger (see sketch 49)

17 THE STREET – 9 September 1865

De Lacy Cottage

De Lacy Cottage dates to the 16th century or possibly earlier. The gabled porch is a 19th-century addition. Ye Olde Cruck House / De Lacy Hall to the south was constructed during the 15th and 18th centuries. It may have been the home of William De Mallett, falconer to Earl Clifford in 1460. There is evidence of it being used as a smokehouse, not only by Charles Neale, pork butcher, at the time of the sketch, but perhaps also in connection with the Severn fishing trade.

Charles Neale

Charles Neale (*c*.1821–1903) was born in Frampton, the son of a gamekeeper who later became a butcher. His mother died in January 1865 and it was around that time that Charles moved to De Lacy Cottage, although he was possibly running his shop from Ye Olde Cruck House prior to that date. The sketch shows what appear to be sides of bacon hung up in the shop. Variously described as a pork butcher and bacon curer, he supplied the Clifford family with spareribs, griskin (the lean part of a loin of pork), lard, sides of bacon, pigs' heads and sausages. Charles was also briefly a beer retailer, which was hardly surprising, for in 1858 he had married Emma, the daughter of Peter Coole who kept *The Three Horseshoes*.

> For some two months past, a juvenile drum and fife band, composed of the boys of the National school, has been organized, under the patronage of the vicar and the leading families of the place, and under the superintendence of Mr. Charles Neale. On Wednesday night they paraded the village, and played a variety of airs in capital style. We hope to have the pleasure of hearing the little men frequently during the winter months. Their efficiency reflects great credit on their able and indefatigable teacher.

Gloucester Journal, 19 September 1863

Charles Neale was a popular character in the village during the 1860s, conducting many of the musical groups.

Hampden Wotton (see sketch 47); William Hart (see sketch 49)

18   THE STREET (EAST) – 15 September 1865

William Merrett

William Merrett, born *c*.1791 in Standish, married in 1813 a local girl, Ann Ayland, who bore him several children.

William was a carpenter and by 1861 they had moved to the house shown. He remained there until his death in 1872, some 10 years after his wife. The parish magazine records his death: 'our aged parishioner was removed after a long and wearing sickness'.

Elizabeth Hadley

There were two women called Elizabeth Hadley in Frampton of roughly the same age and since the caption shows 'B Hadley' perhaps this one was known as Betty.

According to the Chapel's Minute Book, Elizabeth Hadley was born in 1789 and baptised at the chapel the same year, the daughter of Samuel and Ann Clutterbuck. Her first husband, John Harper, died shortly after the birth of their son George, little more than a year after their marriage. Elizabeth's second marriage was not successful, for her husband 'went from home one day and did not return, nor did she ever hear anything of him. She was thus left with two additional sons but under this heavy trial she was divinely supported and had the practical

Sept. 15th 1865.   W. Merrett.   B.H.d.

sympathy of many friends.' At the time of this sketch, Elizabeth Hadley was working as a needlewoman, no longer in need of the parochial relief which she had required during the previous decades. For many years she lived in the household of her friend Ann Russell (see sketch 5), after whose death in 1882 she lived with her eldest son in Painswick. Elizabeth Hadley died in 1886 aged almost 97. At that time her son wrote that she had died from 'softening of the brain'. She had personally known the great nonconformist preacher Rowland Hill who had been so influential in the building of the chapel at Frampton.

William Dowdeswell Orchard

William Dowdeswell Orchard was born *c*.1796 in Slimbridge; Dowdeswell being his mother's maiden name. After marrying Hannah Newcombe the couple had several children and for a while ran the *George Hotel* at Frocester, a busy coaching inn, where their son Joseph Dowdeswell Orchard (see sketch 16) was born. He was also a farmer. William and Hannah spent the years of their retirement in Frampton, and following William's death in 1876 Hannah left this cottage to live with her daughter Mary and son-in-law Walter Hitchings (see sketch 47).

FRAMPTON-ON-SEVERN, GLOUCESTERSHIRE.
Very desirable Freehold Investments.
TO BE SOLD BY AUCTION,
By HUMPHRYS and SONS
At the BELL HOTEL, FRAMPTON-ON-SEVERN, on Wednesday, the 6th of March, 1867, at four o'clock in the afternoon, subject to Conditions which will then be produced,—

THE following VALUABLE FREEHOLD DWELLING-HOUSES, GARDENS, and PREMISES, in Two Lots, viz. :—

Lot 1.—All that substantially Brick-built DWELLING-HOUSE, consisting of three Sitting Rooms, five Bedchambers, Brewhouse, and Out-offices ; together with large GARDEN, as now marked out, lying behind the same, in the occupation of Mr. William Merrett, Carpenter.

This Lot, having the excellent frontage of about 50 feet to the Turnpike-road, offers every facility for Business purposes.

Lot 2.—All those Two Brick-built COTTAGES, with the GARDENS and Appurtenances thereto, adjoining Lot 1, in the occupation of Messrs. Fredericks and Orchard.

There is a Pump and Well of excellent Water on each of the above Lots.

For further particulars, and to view, apply to Mr. Hathaway, the Proprietor, near the Premises ; the Auctioneers, Stroud ; or Mr. Adey, Solicitor, Wotton-under-Edge.

Gloucester Journal, 23 February 1867

Perry. J.Hawker. Evans E.Morgan Woolle Burr. Allen.

Perry

In all probability this was the family of Philip G. Perry, a carpenter and joiner who appears to have spent a brief time in Frampton *c.*1865, when his daughter Athalina was born, before returning on a more permanent basis around 1870. In the interim they had lived in his home village of Whitminster.

John Hawker

John Hawker (*c.*1803-78) from Newnham was one of several blacksmiths in Frampton. His wife Ann came from either Kidderminster or Coventry. Of their two sons, Edwin, the youngest, followed his father's trade whilst Charles, the eldest, became a carpenter. Later in life Edwin was assistant overseer and deputy registrar. They moved to this house during the early 1860s, John and Edwin remaining after Ann's death in 1867.

John Evans, Edward Morgan, Samuel Wooles, John Burr and Amelia Allen (see sketch 19).

19   THE STREET (EAST) – undated (probably September 1865)

Tudor Cottage
Built most probably in the 16th century, Tudor Cottage has a jettied gable projecting over the pavement.

John Evans

John Evans (*c.*1823-98) may have moved to Tudor Cottage after the death of the previous occupant, Mary Ann Davis, in 1852. He and his wife Louisa were both born in Frampton, and

they spent the early days of their married life with Louisa's mother, Ann Burman, in Falfield Cottage situated almost opposite.

They had at least eight children, and it seems likely that several of the daughters went into domestic service away from Frampton, variously marrying a railway clerk from Birmingham, a cloth designer from Yorkshire and a police constable from Pembrokeshire. If the girls did travel they would have found their father's trade of carpenter most useful, for no maid leaving home for a position could go away without a wooden box containing her meagre possessions. Much of John Evans' work was with John Millard (of Woodbine Cottage) on the various farms in the village where they carried out general maintenance, fence and gate building etc. They charged 6 shillings a day between them; their bills often being paid three or six months in arrears.

Malthouse Cottage (now Bokhara)
The cottage shown in the sketch probably dates to the 17th century. It was demolished in the 1930s and rebuilt using most of the original materials.

Edward Morgan

Edward Morgan's house was known as Malthouse Cottage, having been the home of a maltster until the mid 1830s when it was sold, the advertisement indicating that the property was suitable for any business requiring room. As a considerable part of the purchase money could remain on mortgage, Edward Morgan took the opportunity to buy it for his young family and flourishing business. A builder and stone mason, Edward was born in Frampton *c.*1800 and during the 1860s he was employing five men and one boy.

Edward married twice and was deacon at the chapel from 1844 until his death in 1868. He

was one of the first scholars at the Chapel's Sunday School at a time when most youngsters in Frampton were uneducated, and having seen the importance of learning he later became a teacher there himself. One of his sons was blind from the age of ten but found employment as an organist.

Buckholdt Cottages

This set of three cottages was built in the late 18th or early 19th century.

Samuel Wooles

Samuel Wooles, shoemaker, was born in the village *c*.1793. In 1835 the Overseers of the Poor tried to pursue Samuel and his brothers in an effort to compel them to maintain their parents, who were costing the parish 3 shillings a week in poor relief. It is likely that this cottage was the Wooles' family home prior to Samuel and Eliza's marriage in 1838. The couple do not appear to have had any children and when Samuel fell ill just before the end of his life, Eliza may not have managed the journey to see him at the Wheatenhurst Union Workhouse situated in the neighbouring parish of Eastington. At the Workhouse there was accommodation not only for the paupers and lunatics, but also the sick such as Samuel Wooles. They both died in 1871.

John Burr

John Burr (*c*.1806-77) and his family lived in the middle part of Buckholdt Cottages from sometime between 1851 and 1861. A cabinet maker by trade, he was born in Westbury-on-Severn.

S. Bowles.

John Burr was a rather jolly character, entering into every aspect of village life. During the celebrations of the Royal Wedding of the Prince of Wales in 1863 he took it upon himself to act as town crier and supervised the various races that took place during the afternoon's festivities. These included the popular races of the day: the three legged race, hurdles and jumping in sacks.

As secretary to the Female and Male Septennial Benefit Clubs for more than thirty years he commanded respect from his fellow villagers, and as a tribute to him the members of those clubs erected a 'handsome monument in the churchyard' in 'grateful remembrance of his services'. Some years earlier he had presented Miss Anne Watts with an illuminated address in recognition of her works towards the two Benefit Clubs; the handsome frame of carved oak, skilfully inlaid and enriched with sacred emblems of faith, in gold and red and blue, having been his work. In 1854 he had tendered along with Edward Hewlett, a carpenter in the village, for the contract to replace the pews in the church.

John Burr was a census enumerator from 1841 until 1871 and also secretary to the Frampton Vessel Owners' Insurance Club in the 1860s. Along with several other members of the community he also collected Land Tax from the villagers during the 1860s. John Burr won numerous prizes for his flowers, fruit and vegetables at the Frampton and Fretherne Cottage Gardeners' Society shows in the 1860s, so he must have found some time to relax in his garden despite a heavy schedule of other duties.

Amelia Allen

Amelia Allen, a straw bonnet maker and dressmaker born *c.*1818 in Frampton, was living in this cottage in 1841 with her mother and grandfather, Sarah Allen and William Chappell. By 1851

she was head of the household and appears to have lived mainly on her own in Buckholdt Cottages until her death in 1880.

One night, in December 1862, Amelia Allen was burgled. As was the custom, the parish magazine did not name either the 'lonely defenceless neighbour' or the 'cowardly thief' although the *Gloucester Journal* was more than happy to enlighten its readers with the details of those involved.

HOUSE BREAKING.—*Charles Dunn*, a labourer, of Frampton, was charged with breaking into the house of Miss Amelia Allen, at Frampton, on Sunday evening last, during her absence at chapel, and stealing 14s. in silver, and ten new pennies. P.C. Bishop deposed to arresting the prisoner, and finding in his possession 6s. in silver, and 9d. in copper. Among the money was a florin, and some new pence, similar to what was stolen from the house; and he had compared the prisoner's shoes with the foot-prints on Miss Allen's premises, which were very peculiar, and they corresponded. He had found prisoner was drinking at Lodge's beer-house, near Miss Allen's, until after six o'clock on Sunday night, when he left for nearly an hour, and returned to the beer-house in a different dress.

The Bench said they did not consider the evidence sufficient to commit Dunn for trial, and should discharge him, at the same time recommended the police to keep a watch upon him.

Gloucester Journal, 27 December 1862

20 BUCKHOLDT – 13 September 1865

The original part of Buckholdt was built in the middle of the 18th century. Enlarged to the south in the late 18th century, it was again extended to the south and rear in the 19th century. At the time of the sketch the property was known as Buckle-bridge House in recognition of its proximity to the nearby Buckle Brook which flows under The Street.

Samuel Rowles

Samuel Rowles (*c.*1799–1886) was a ship owner and merchant from Arlingham, the brother of

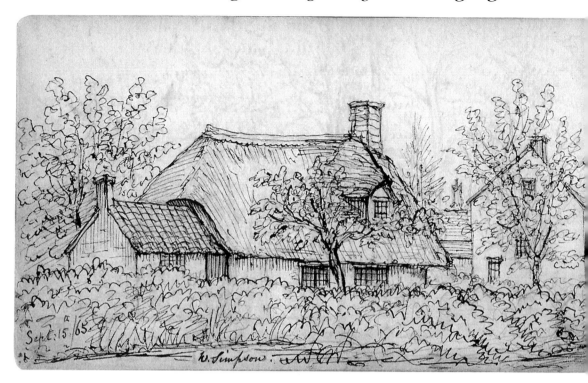

Edwin (see sketch 51). Their father was a waterman and the two brothers benefited from the opening of the Gloucester and Berkeley Canal, which coincided with the earlier part of their careers. The 1860s were a particularly busy period in the canal's history and the Rowles did very well for themselves.

It is possible that Buckholdt was extended in 1841 for it was unoccupied at the time of the census that year, Samuel living further down The Street in Yew Tree House, which he probably also owned. Once the work at Buckholdt was complete, it was said that Samuel could look out of his upstairs windows and see his many boats plying up and down the canal. A successful trader, he dealt in bricks, tiles and coal as well as other commodities. He rented a brickpit from the Cliffords near Splatt Bridge. (It is not clear from his account to Jane French at Church Farm in 1871 whether the 750 bricks she bought for 16s. 6d. were from his brickyard near Splatt or brought in by barge.)

Samuel's second wife came from either south Gloucestershire or Wiltshire and the household always included at least one servant; more when their children were young. Elizabeth was much loved in the village and when Samuel died she took over his 'extensive' business as a stone merchant at Frampton and Chepstow owning a large number of vessels.

Samuel Rowles was churchwarden of St Mary's Church several times and he supplied fuel for the soup kitchen that was set up each winter for the poor of the village. A supporter of the Royal family he bedecked his gateway with flowers and 'a loyal motto surmounted by a floral crown of great elegance' to mark the wedding of the Prince of Wales in 1863.

Samuel was also a prime mover in the nine-year campaign (1859-68) to have the privately owned Whitminster Lane transferred to public ownership.

Stinchcombe hill in R.A. Hierons the distance. Entrance to the Narles. ML

21   THE STREET LOOKING SOUTH JUST AFTER THE LYCHGATE
– 15 September 1865

Site of Brooklyn
This cottage has been demolished.

William Simpson

William Simpson was born *c.*1806 in South Cerney and came to Frampton in the late 1830s with his wife Hannah and their eldest daughter. They moved to this cottage on the eastern side of The Street (situated just south of Buckholdt) sometime between 1851 and 1861 and William endeavoured to ensure the best possible future for their six surviving children by sending them to the National School.

The youngest, Fanny, appears to have become disenchanted with school after she reached the top class when she was 13. Regularly chastised for poor attendance and lack of effort, her school career ended with the following entry in the logbook: 'Oct. 27th 1864 – Blew up F Simpson this morning for idleness and backwardness and indifference about her lessons. Gave her to understand we would have no dross here. If she didn't choose to work she had better stay at home.' Fanny left school that day and went into service, possibly in London, for she later married a French polisher from Bethnal Green named Joseph Dean. Two of the other daughters became dressmakers, one of whom was unmarried when she provided the Simpsons with two granddaughters in 1863 and 1867. The family were kind and stood by her so that she was spared the indignity of the workhouse.

William was an agricultural labourer all his life and was still working well into his seventies. Hannah took in laundry once her family had grown up and left home. Both remained in the cottage until their respective deaths, William in 1887 and Hannah five years later, in 1892.

The Summer House

Richard Heiron

Born in Frampton *c.*1805, Richard Heiron married Mary Guy, also from Frampton, in 1831. They moved to The Summer House, which Richard bought in 1838 for £200 from Henry Clifford Clifford, and it was from there that he also ran his butcher's business, selling a variety of meats. The couple had four children.

It seems that during the 1860s no concert in Frampton was complete without Richard Heiron. His bass voice rendered solos from *Judas Maccabaeus* by Handel with 'great energy and precision' and he delighted in performing such songs as *The Organ Grinder* in character, causing much merriment amongst the audience who regularly demanded encores.

He died in 1876, from which time another butcher, John Gerrish, took over the property and business.

22 THE STREET (EAST) – 18 September 1865

Cottages before Wild Goose Cottage
These three cottages have since been demolished.

Cooper's, Wright, Deborah Brazington.   Wright - F. Daw. Collett. W. Cole. Sept. 18-

Charles Evans

Charles Evans was born in Frampton around the turn of the century and was a schoolmaster for most of his working life, except for a short while at the beginning of the 1850s when he was clerk to the Trustees of Roads. He and his wife, Mary Ann, had nine children and moved to this cottage between 1841 and 1851.

Charles Evans was blind for the final 16 years of his life and probably one of the last tasks he performed fully sighted was in 1851 when he was one of the enumerators for the census.

> **Death** – January 17th, at Frampton-on-Severn, after a long and painful illness, of disease of the brain, borne with Christian fortitude, Mr. Charles Evans, late schoolmaster, aged 68 years.
>
> *Gloucester Journal*, 2 February 1867

Alice Elizabeth Evans, one of Charles' daughters was infant teacher at the National School from 1867 until her premature death in 1875, at the age of 26. For much of her time at the school she suffered from ill health; she even made a visit to Cheltenham in 1869 to seek medical advice. Miss Evans was very popular with the infants and many of them stayed away from school when she was absent through illness. A valentine was pushed under her classroom door on one occasion, although the school logbook does not indicate whether it was from a pupil or an adult admirer. 'Her amiable temper and unvarying kindness to the little ones under her care had endeared her to them all, for she herself had loved them dearly, and bore with them patiently, and carried them in her heart to the very last, some of her latest spoken words being the expression of an earnest desire for their welfare.'

William Daw

The sketch shows the occupier as 'G Daw', but William Daw was the head of the household on both the 1861 and 1871 censuses. Later William and his family moved to Beehive Cottage on the western side of The Street. He was born in Frampton *c.*1829 and married Charlotte Gibbs in 1853.

William worked as a waterman, obtaining his Seaman's Register Ticket at Cardiff when he was sixteen. Work as a waterman was hard and sailing the waters of the Bristol Channel and Severn Estuary could be dangerous, a fact known only too well to William whose younger brother Caleb had been knocked overboard by a rope and drowned aged only 17 or 18.

William Daw jointly owned a trow called *Happy-go-Lucky* between 1864 and 1887 with his friend Reuben Charles. She had been built in Bridgnorth in 1841 and lasted 73 useful years before being lost in 1914. Descendants of William, still living, have a narrowboat of the same name.

The boat's crew generally comprised four men including the master and they would go from port to port taking whatever cargo they could. Coals from South Wales, timber from Bristol, iron ore from the Forest of Dean and bricks from Gloucester were among the loads. Payment was by the trip irrespective of the length of the journey.

The Frampton Vessel Owners' Insurance Club's surviving records for the 1860s are confined to the occasional mention in the parish magazine and *Gloucester Chronicle*. In 1866 the insurance cover for *Happy-go-Lucky* was increased from £100 to £150. The parish magazine of April 1874 gives a good indication of the Club's activities during the 11 years it had existed. In that particular year 64 vessels were covered for sums ranging from £80 to £200. Although the Club provided cover against both shipwreck and the employment of vessels which were not seaworthy, it nevertheless managed good profits and a bonus of 10 per cent on the insured value was paid to members in March 1874. The total cost of losses and expenses since 1863 had amounted to £1,429.

Ann Ayland

Giles Ayland, a waterman from Arlingham, died aged 64 in April 1865, so when the sketch was drawn only his widow Ann (born *c.*1808 in Frampton) was living in this cottage which had been their home since the 1840s. Married in October 1830, their daughter was baptised just two months later, a not uncommon occurrence in those days.

Wild Goose Cottage

Wild Goose Cottage is one of the oldest in the village. Dating possibly from as early as the 14th century, but certainly the 15th century, the central portion would have originally been an open hall to roof height. The roof timbers still bear the marks from the soot and smoke of those times. Sometime later this cottage was divided into three dwellings, each with its own entrance and spiral staircase, the accommodation basically comprising one room downstairs and one room upstairs. Henry Clifford Clifford, the owner, tried unsuccessfully to sell the cottages in 1838 wanting a price of at least £200. The bidding stopped at £100 and the sale was withdrawn.

Charlotte Cooper

John Cooper and his wife Sarah had lived in the northerly end of Wild Goose Cottage from before the days of that sale. After the family had grown up, Charlotte seems to have stayed at home to look after her parents whilst the younger children married and moved away. One son, Joseph, died of smallpox in 1848. Charlotte Cooper's illegitimate son, John Henry, was baptised in 1838 and nine months later Charlotte and her baby spent one day in the Workhouse at Eastington. The last trace of John Henry is on the 1841 census when he was living with the Cooper family.

The Coopers were very poor. John Cooper had been a bricklayer, and after his death in 1852 both Sarah and Charlotte had to find whatever work they could. On the 1861 census they were labourers aged 77 and 47 respectively. Sarah died in February 1865 so the initial 'S' on the sketch appears to be an oversight.

With both her parents dead, Charlotte Cooper left Wild Goose Cottage to become a general servant to Mrs. Ann Watts at The Grange where she was living in 1871, aged 57. The Watts were a generous family, particularly where the poor were concerned, and had perhaps offered her a job out of kindness.

Charlotte returned to Wild Goose Cottage by 1881, but life remained difficult for her and on the 1891 census she was described as 'living on charity'. She died in 1895 aged 81.

Sarah Wright

Sarah Wright, born *c.*1792, possibly in Stroud, was the widow of Richard Wright, a coal hallier (haulier) from Evesham who had died in 1862 aged 85. They lived in the middle part of Wild Goose Cottage from before 1836. Sarah was shown as 'deaf' on the 1851 census but this may have been a temporary disability for no mention of it is made in the later censuses.

Seating in church was allocated according to the owner of the property concerned, and a list drawn up in 1841 still survives. It shows that John Cooper, John Woodman and Richard Wright (the three cottagers at Wild Goose) were given two separate seats in the church and it appears that this was the total allocation between them, the three cottages being treated as a single building. Those unlucky enough not to be given a seat would stand at the back of the church during the services.

Deborah Brazington (or Brazenton)

Deborah Brazington (born *c.*1788) was the widow of Thomas, an agricultural labourer from Harescombe. He probably had a strong accent for the 1851 census records his birthplace as Ascomb. He died in 1864 and she in 1869. Long time tenants of Henry Clifford Clifford, the Brazingtons paid an annual rental for the cottage of £3 0s. 0d. The annual rental for the cottages occupied by Charlotte Cooper and Sarah Wright (above) was £3 1s. 0d. and £4 1s. 0d. respectively.

Cottages on the site of Bendles
These cottages have been demolished.

Thomas Wright

Thomas Wright was a waterman, the son of Sarah Wright (see above) and her husband Richard. Born in Frampton *c.*1819, it is likely that Thomas had met Mary Ann his wife through his work, for she was the daughter of a waterman and came from Bridgwater, a busy port in the 19th century. Their several children were baptised irregularly, some waiting until several years after their birth, perhaps because Thomas' work took him away from home a great deal. Thomas and Mary Ann both died in 1887.

William Brown.   Mrs Goatman.

Francis Daw

Francis Daw was a bricklayer and then builder by trade. Born in Frampton *c.*1810, he married a local girl, Susannah Guy, in 1836 and both were able to sign the register. The couple had nine children, two of whom died in infancy.

The children were all educated at the National School just down the road from their house, although a couple of entries in the school's logbook indicate that their attendance was irregular. Francis and his family moved frequently and were at a different location in the village for each census. He died in 1877.

John Collett

John Collett was variously a labourer and bargeman/mariner, born in Frampton *c.*1815. Both he and his wife Sarah were illegitimate according to their marriage certificate of 1844, and neither they nor their witnesses could sign their names. Two years later their son Charles was born, and he also became a labourer and mariner.

William Cole

William Cole (*c.*1838-1916) was a farm labourer. Born in Frampton, he married Emma Brooks, the daughter of a waterman, in 1862. The couple may have moved into this cottage after their wedding day. Their 11 children were all given second Christian names which had become fashionable by the middle of the 19th century. By 1881 the family had moved to Townfield, presumably needing more space.

W.ᵐ Emerson. J. Hobbs. — *National Schools. Sophys Nettie Vicarage gate.*

23 THE STREET (EAST) including the National School
– undated (probably September 1865)

The Shrubs
The Shrubs may have originally been one house and was probably built during the early 17th century.

William Brown
William Brown (*c.*1797–1881) came from Whitminster and he and his wife Hannah (who was born in Frampton), moved to the northern part of The Shrubs before 1851.

The garden must have looked lovely during William's occupation of The Shrubs, for gardening was not only his trade but also his hobby. He won many prizes during the 1860s at the Frampton and Fretherne Cottage Gardeners' Society shows for his vegetables and fruit. At the first show in 1863 he came second for the 'neatest, best arranged and best cultivated' garden and a year later took first prize in the same category.

Ann Goatman
Ann Goatman was the widow of John Goatman (1790–1862), an agricultural labourer. In 1841 the southern part of The Shrubs had been occupied by Ann Goatman's parents, Thomas and Mary Nurbury. It appears that on Thomas' death in 1843, John Goatman and his wife moved in, Ann's mother remaining with them until she died in 1857 aged 94. Ann had married John Goatman in 1829. He was from Ashleworth and she from Framilode or Frampton (the censuses differ).

Ann Goatman died in 1884 aged 89 at her daughter's home in Gloucester. Her death announcement in the *Gloucester Journal* included a typical phrase of the time: 'Deeply regretted by a large circle of friends'.

Leyland

This house had been the schoolmaster's dwelling from sometime before 1851 (it was unoccupied in 1841) until between 1871 and 1881.

Richard Emerson

When the sketch was drawn Richard Emerson was master of the National School. Born in Cumberland *c*.1819, Richard Emerson had a young family when he arrived in Frampton in the very late 1850s, and his wife Sarah taught sewing to the girls at the school.

Richard Emerson worked hard to achieve what he could with the children. Many of them attended infrequently, with bad weather, the harvest and outbreaks of smallpox and measles being the main reasons for absence. His frustrations at the lack of progress made by some children are evident in the logbook, but so is his pleasure at their achievements. Funding of the school was largely dependent on the Government grant made each year, and the level of this was set following an annual assessment by HM Inspector. His visits were feared by staff and pupils alike, although for much of the 1860s HMI J.R. Byrne appeared a kindly gentleman, sympathetic to the conditions under which the school functioned. The Report of 1865 is as follows:

> The school maintains its well deserved character for sound teaching in the elementary subjects. The casualties have been very few and those chiefly in arithmetic and in the second standard, while those who have passed have done in many instances very creditably. The children are singularly neat, orderly and attentive to their work. The show of needlework is very far above the average both in quantity and quality, and the first and second classes appear fairly well acquainted with the facts of the Old Testament although slow to comprehend and answer questions. They should be taught generally to speak out loud and distinctly, and more time might be devoted to their instruction in scripture, geography and history without injury to their prospects in the elementary examination and with great advantage to the elder scholars, if it tends to cultivate their understanding and give expression to their reading.

Elizabeth Emerson, Richard's daughter, became pupil teacher at the school. This meant she taught the younger children, whilst still receiving educational instruction herself.

Richard Emerson's career had previously taken him to Douglas, Isle of Man, and Epperstone, Nottinghamshire. The last entry in the logbook relating to him was written in the hand of the vicar: 'Sept. 6th 1867 – The school was dismissed and Mr Emerson left.' (There had been no indication of his likely departure in the records.)

Stephen Smith

Stephen Smith, born *c*.1838 in Gloucester, succeeded Richard Emerson as master of the National School in 1868 and lived in the above house. A glance at the school logbook reveals a very different character and the children must have viewed their new master with some trepidation during the first few weeks after his arrival. On only his second day he wrote in the logbook: 'Children give me great provocation by their evil habit of continually talking' and he handed out many punishments for this and lateness, regularly using the phrase 'I was obliged to punish them'. His first annual inspection was far from successful as the children struggled to understand what was required of them both in terms of discipline and learning. The Government grant, at £37 8s. 8d., was almost £12 lower than that given for the previous year.

The school did, however, thrive under the leadership of Stephen Smith as he gradually persuaded parents to send their children more regularly. In the first 18 months average daily attendance rose from 76 to 120, although this figure still fluctuated at times of harvest, bad weather and illness. The Government grant in 1869 was £61 13s. 4d. reflecting the better attendance of the children and their increased ability.

Stephen Smith, like his predecessor, worked hard for the National School making the best of the limited resources available. 'I pasted some tables on some cards and put the 3rd and 4th classes to learn them' is a typical entry in the logbook.

At his departure in 1873 he was described as 'popular', and 'the teachers and scholars combined to purchase a handsome bible as a token of their esteem and good will towards him'.

Yew Tree House

Thomas Hobbs

Thomas Hobbs (c.1824-77) moved to this property between 1851 and 1861. A labourer when he married Elizabeth Rea in 1848, he was arguably Frampton's best example of a 'self-made man'. Variously a waterman, coal merchant and barge owner in the three successive censuses (1851-1871) he owned at least three trows (*Longney Lass*, *Friends* and *Druid*) during the 1860s. These vessels plied the Bristol Channel, River Severn and Gloucester and Berkeley Canal between the ports of Cardiff, Newport, Lydney, Gloucester, Bristol and Bridgwater. On board would be the master and two or three seamen of varying ages. Following Thomas' death, Elizabeth continued to own and run *Longney Lass*. She lived in Yew Tree House until some time after the 1881 census.

Thomas and Elizabeth Hobbs had 13 children. The Hobbs family's approach to education was very mixed. Orlando, the eldest, became a ship's carpenter having finished school at the age of 14. The second son, Thomas, left to follow the same trade aged 11 years and 2 months, but soon returned for an intermittent education until leaving to be a butcher 18 months later. A couple of the daughters are mentioned as infrequent attenders in the school's logbook.

However, the third son, William, had a very colourful and long connection with the National School, eventually becoming its master from 1881 until 1886. William's early days at the school are not documented, the first entry being his appointment as monitor in October 1867. The following year he rose to the position of pupil teacher and was apprenticed to the school for five years. He must have tested the master's patience on many occasions for he was often late and sometimes did not turn up at all, particularly if there was a coursing match in the village or the hounds were out. His biggest failing, however, was his predisposition towards corporal punishment. He was frequently reported by parents for beating their children. This continued in later life for in 1882, soon after William became the master of the National School, he wrote the following entry: 'Thrashed a boy for gross insubordination. Gave him 6 cuts on the back with the cane.' He was reported to the magistrates, who acquitted him. He had learnt a salutary lesson, for corporal punishment was never mentioned again in the logbook during his time as master. Indeed, the school flourished under his leadership and was assessed 'excellent'.

National School

The National Society for the Education of the Poor in the Principles of the Established Church was founded in 1811. It assisted with the development of Church of England schools by allowing grants to pay the teaching staff and assisting with building projects. These establishments became known as 'National Schools'.

The National School in Frampton was built in 1842 and catered for both boys and girls. The vicar was a regular visitor rehearsing the children in the Catechism and conducting their prayers. The main school holiday in the summer, known as Harvest Holiday, varied in timing each year to coincide with the ripening of the crops.

A number of the older children acted as monitors. They could be as young as twelve. It was their job to oversee the work of a group of younger children (known as a division). At the end of the school day or at lunchtime the monitors would receive their own tuition in readiness for the following day's lessons. The most senior of these monitors would be the pupil teacher who was apprenticed, from the age of 13, for five years. A pupil teacher presented himself or herself for examination at the end of his apprenticeship, and if successful gained his Queen's Scholarship enabling him to attend a training college for three years.

The school bell was an essential item in the 1860s, as many people did not possess a household clock. It could be heard all over the village summoning the children to their lessons. Lateness was often punished and youngsters scurried along the road in the morning and afternoon in an effort to reach their classes on time. Some, however, were perpetual offenders and would arrive late frequently, despite the thrashing or beating they might receive from the master. The school day started at 9a.m. and ran until 12 noon when there was a two-hour break for lunch. This gave the children sufficient time to return home for their meal, although some preferred to stay and eat their bread and cheese at school. Afternoon lessons were from 2p.m. until 4p.m., although sometimes the school finished earlier during the winter months and later when the master felt the children were behind with their studies. Detentions of either 30 minutes or an hour were frequent and without prior announcement.

From 1861 Her Majesty's School Inspector visited each year to examine the children's work. Prior to these visits the master would plead with the children to arrive at school on time, tidy and clean. Grants were calculated based on the pupil's results and much effort was put in each year to obtain the maximum possible achievement. The master was also paid by results. Performance at Frampton's National School varied greatly throughout the 1860s and depended mostly on the ability of the pupils to pass these annual examinations and attendance. It was an unfair system for in one particular year the grant was severely cut because many of the children were absent from school with measles on the day of the examination, and those who did attend were either recovering from the illness or feeling its first effects.

Each year the vicar published extracts from the report of the School Inspector in the parish magazine. Some years there was praise for needlework, the infants or a particular academic subject, but more often than not the message was to try harder. Generally throughout the country School Inspectors kept grants to a minimum thereby placing a greater burden on the wealthier members of the parishes to ensure the financial viability of their schools. Frampton was no exception to this. The main subscribers, apart from the local gentry and clergy, were the farmers, who saw it as their duty to provide the opportunity of education to the children of their employees. The fee for attending school was 1d. per week until 1866, when it was doubled to 2d. The abstract of the School Accounts which appeared in the 1868 parish magazine shows just how tight the budget was (see opposite).

Much was done locally and nationally to encourage children to receive an education. Forster's Education Act of 1870 provided that elementary schools should be established in areas where school provision was insufficient, but this would have had little effect on Frampton with its National, Chapel and Private Schools. The Act did, however, focus attention on the need for

ABSTRACT OF SCHOOL ACCOUNTS.

INCOME.	£	s.	d.	EXPENDITURE.	£	s.	d.
Mr. Clifford	30	0	0	Salaries of Teachers	97	0	5
Mrs. H. Clifford	8	0	0	„ Assistants... ...	26	8	9
Executors of the late Mr.				„ Pupil Teachers...	2	6	2
Clifford	20	0	0	„ Monitors	1	12	8
Mr. J. Watts	12	10	0	Books, &c.	3	6	10½
Mrs. Watts	2	0	0	Fuel, &c.	3	10	9
Mr. T. Watts	1	10	0	Repairs, &c.	2	9	11
Mr. S. Rowles	1	0	0	Rent	10	0	0
Mr. and Mrs. E. Rowles ...	1	0	0				
The Vicar	4	0	0		146	15	6½
Mr. Bubb	0	10	0				
Mr. Turner	0	10	0				
Mrs. Russell	0	10	0				
Mr. Hill...	0	10	0				
Miss Barnard	0	5	0				
Mr. Hulbert	0	2	6				
Total Subscriptions ...	82	7	6				
Church Collection...	4	14	6				
Penny Readings	3	17	0				
School Pence...	28	16	8				
Books sold to Children ...	1	3	0	Due to Treasurer last year	18	16	6
Government Grant	45	5	2	Balance in hand now	0	11	9½
	£166	3	10		£166	3	10

an education and the problems of child labour. In 1872 the question was addressed in the parish magazine by highlighting the nearby village of Upton St Leonards where the principal farmers and employers asked the schoolmaster to select two boys who would work on alternate days for the wages of a single boy, thereby enabling each of the boys to attend school. The vicar of Frampton felt this to be good practice and recommended it to his own parishioners.

Education did not become compulsory until 1880 and, even then, parents were expected to pay fees until they were eventually abolished in 1891. Most families in Frampton managed to send their children to school during the 1860s, although some of the families at Fromebridge remained illiterate.

The schoolroom was used for meetings and concerts, for there was no parish hall in the village during the 1860s. Sometimes the children were lucky enough to have a half day holiday while the room was prepared for an evening event. Extra chairs were hired, having been brought on a wagon. A platform was built to enable the performers to be seen, and the piano was tuned in readiness.

Gloucester Journal, 9 August 1862

Afterwards great efforts were made to ensure that the room was cleared and swept in time for school the next day.

Concerts by the choir consisted of sacred music for the first half of the evening followed by secular songs after the interval. Other popular events were evenings of music and readings where small groups of parishioners would perform. Occasionally singers would come from outside the village such as 'Morgan's Little Men', a popular group of young singers and instrumentalists who were based in Gloucester.

On Monday, Wednesday and Friday evenings, from 7p.m. until 9p.m. Night School met in the schoolroom; the charge towards the heat and light increasing from 2d. to 3d. per week in 1868.

Lectures were also given in the schoolroom, notably on Australia in 1869 by John Watts, brother of the village doctor Thomas Watts, who made occasional visits to Frampton. Although his first wife is commemorated on a window in the church, John Watts lived for many years in Queensland, and was a member of the Australian Parliament. At the time of his second marriage in 1866 he was Minister of Works for Queensland. In his talk he described sheep shearing at Christmas on his large estate, which no doubt fascinated the folk of Frampton.

THE MARRIAGE OF THE PRINCE OF WALES – Tuesday 10 March 1863

There was much interest regarding the marriage of Edward VII, the Prince of Wales, to Princess Alexandra of Denmark. The whole country was filled with excitement and celebrations were widespread.

For many days prior to the wedding the villagers of Frampton had made their preparations by entwining evergreens into decorations and making up wedding favours. On the morning itself the village presented a 'most cheerful and pleasing aspect' with flags and streamers everywhere. Many of the houses were 'tastefully decorated with arches, festoons, mottoes and devices', but the main point of attraction was opposite the Mechanics' Institute on the green where a marquee had been erected under the supervision of William Wood, for consuming the meal later in the day.

On Monday last a tree was planted on the Green, commemoration of the marriage of His Royal Highne the Prince of Wales. At one o'clock the children the National Schools assembled at their school, a shortly after two o'clock marched up the village, carr ing banners and flags. On arriving on the Green th were joined by the children of the Congregation Schools, with the Rev. W. Lewis, and then march to the Court House. After singing "God bless t Prince of Wales," and the National Anthem, each chi received a medal, and giving three hearty cheers, th proceeded to the scene of the tree planting, headed a cart, containing the tree—a flourishing young oa A large concourse of persons were assembled to witne the planting. When completed and fenced roun and named the "Alexandra Oak," three cheers we heartily given, and the assemblage dispersed.

Gloucester Journal, 11 April 1863

Early in the morning guns were fired followed by the ringing of the bells at St Mary's. At half past nine the children from the National School assembled and attended a service at the church. Afterwards they marched to The Vicarage where they were presented with banners, streamers and white favours. The vicar and his wife then accompanied the procession through the village to the green where they met with the children from the Congregational Schools who were similarly carrying flags and favours and being headed by their own minister and his wife, the Rev. and Mrs. Lewis. The procession, then led by the village band, moved to Frampton Court where the children formed a semicircle and sang the National Anthem and a new song especially written by Brinley Richards for the occasion 'God bless the Prince of Wales'.

The children (numbering approximately 240) marched to the marquee and sat down to a substantial meal of roast beef and plum pudding, over which the vicar and minister presided. Shortly before midday, Lieutenant Sumner, in full uniform, fired a salute of 21 guns. The children then made their way out onto The Green to enjoy themselves whilst the adults took their places in the marquee. During the morning two sheep, provided by the local butchers George Hobbs and Richard Heiron and each weighing a hundredweight, had been roasted on spits. Peter Coole, the landlord of *The Three Horseshoes* (and according to one contemporary account the Mayor of Frampton), had supervised the cooking before singing his favourite ditty 'Let us live in hopes the times will mend'. The adults then 'speedily demolished' their meal, giving credence to the apparently well known axiom 'that Frampton air produces appetite'. Food was sent to the sick and bedridden thanks to the kind forethought of the organisers of the event.

The afternoon was spent taking part in various races (hurdles, jumping in sacks and flat races etc.) together with other athletic sports, under the superintendence of the local veterinary surgeon, William Coole, with John Burr acting as town crier. Tea followed in the marquee where again rich and poor fraternised. In the evening there was a brilliant display of fireworks consisting of sky rockets, wheel rockets and balloons etc., followed by a large bonfire of brushwood and tar barrels.

The whole event, masterminded by the vicar, was much enjoyed and was typical of the celebrations taking place all over the country that day. Expenditure was as follows:

	£.	s.	d.
To Children's Dinner, with Bread and Beer	8	19	0½
Two Sheep and Thirty Loaves, for Men's Dinner ...	7	17	4¼
Wedding Favours and Pins	2	7	9
Band	1	0	0
Bonfire	0	7	6
Fireworks	2	6	6
Printing	0	4	6
Labour	1	12	3
	£24	14	11

24 VICARAGE LANE – undated (probably 23 September 1865)

Primrose Cottage

Ann Guy

Ann Guy was born *c.*1812 at Frampton and appears to have moved to the western side of Primrose Cottage following the death of her 'husband' Thomas in 1849. (They had not been legally wed because Thomas had previously been married to Ann's younger sister, and although she had died it was forbidden by law at that time to marry your deceased wife's sister. In practice most people turned a blind eye to anyone marrying in this way particularly as it often provided a practical solution for a widower left with young children. The law was repealed in the early 1900s.)

Ann brought up both her own son Frederick and his half-brother Thomas, but life was not at all easy for her. The family received parochial relief for a while as Ann struggled to find the money to feed, clothe and educate the boys. She worked as a laundress probably taking in

washing from the other villagers and would have spent her days soaking and soaping the clothes and linen, rinsing and putting it through the mangle or wringer, starching and drying, and then lastly ironing. It was tiring, hard work, and it must have been difficult for Ann to dry the washing in her tiny cottage during the cold and wet days.

Henry Daw

Henry Daw (c.1807-74) was born in Frampton and married Elizabeth Birt in 1828. The couple had lived in the eastern part of Primrose Cottage from before 1841 with their several children, one of whom, Caleb, was drowned in the River Severn.

Henry Daw, a shoemaker, had recently been widowed when the sketch was drawn although he later appears to have remarried.

to be well nigh if not entirely solvent.

A MAN DROWNED IN THE SEVERN.—A waterman named Caleb Daw was on Monday se'nnight drowned in the Severn. He was engaged with others in a boat towing a vessel, when, in consequence of the boat taking the "slack tide," and the vessel being in the "strong tide," the deceased was caught by the rope and knocked overboard. A rope was thrown to him, but he could not catch hold; he held by the "thought" for three or four minutes, and then sank. The body was not recovered until Tuesday last, when a waterman named James White found it floating on the river, about half-a-mile of Beachley. An inquest was held upon it yesterday, (Friday,) before J. Lovegrove, Esq. and a verdict of accidentally drowned was returned.

COOLNESS.—The *Stroud Free Press* this week contains

Gloucester Journal, 29 July 1854

Shakespeare Cottage

George Evans

George Evans was a waterman, and when his first wife died leaving a young family he employed a housekeeper, Mary Gully, to look after his children whilst he was away at sea. Having been born c.1790, she was approximately the same age as George, and once the children had grown up the couple married in 1849. His four sons all followed their father and became mariners starting their careers on the Gloucester and Berkeley Canal and then progressing to coastal and deep waters. Later three of his grandsons became 'seamen of comparable devotion, linking the great days of sail to steam, the bustle of Gloucester Docks to the greatness of the Tyne'. George and Mary both died in 1867 and the cottage was then occupied by Maria, daughter of George, and her husband, Richard James Winter.

Rachel Mills

Mark Mills, the son of John (see sketch 28), was born c.1829 in Frampton and married Rachel Woodward from Dursley in 1857. The Mills moved to this cottage c.1863. At the time Mark was a waterman and, as the sketch is captioned R. Mills, was presumably away at sea when this sketch was drawn. By 1871 Mark had changed to the occupation of his father, who was by now a bricklayer, and he spent much of his time working with Giles Wilkins, another bricklayer/builder, at a wage of 3s. 4d. a day. The couple had six surviving children and the eldest two sons also became bricklayers.

Accord to the school logbook, nearly every family in the parish had an allotment, and the Mills were no exception, Mark renting his from Henry Clifford Clifford for a guinea per annum. The families mainly used their allotments for the growing of potatoes and children would be away from school for a couple of weeks a year helping firstly with the planting, and later the digging of the crop. Other vegetables and fruit were grown too, and the gardeners were no doubt encouraged by their successes in the Frampton and Fretherne Cottage Gardeners' Society annual shows that took place in the mid-1860s. Rachel and Mark Mills died in 1894 and 1895 respectively.

William Causon

William Causon (or Causton as the earlier records show) was an agricultural labourer from Twyning, near Tewkesbury. According to the 1841 census, William (c.1817–85) was employed as a male servant to Walter Longney the farmer at Tanhouse Farm. In the village he met and married Eliza Mills, sister of Mark Mills (above), in 1843, which may have been the time that they came to live in this cottage.

William and Eliza had four children. Typically one of them, Laura, is noted in the National School logbook as having been admitted just after her third birthday. She moved to the upper school aged five and a half. Laura would have been among the scholars to celebrate the anniversary of the Restoration of King Charles II on 29 May 1867 by wearing a twig of oak in their buttonholes, the school being decorated with boughs. Just six years later the school logbook records that the children 'intend keeping up the day as May Pole Day'.

Barradell

This was likely to have been the home of Elizabeth Barradell and her son Robert. She was probably born in Wiltshire c.1794 and died in 1886. Robert was a tinker, and later a scissors and knife grinder, born in Upton

> *Robert Barradell*, a labourer, and *Henry Hobbs*, of Frampton, were charged with stealing 139lbs. weight of lead, the property of H. C. Clifford, Esq., Frampton Court. On the 1st instant Barradell went to Mr. Yeend, at Gloucester, and sold the lead; most of it was melted down.—Mr. H. Brimmell, in Mr. Yeend's employ, weighed the lead, and asked the prisoner where he had it from? he replied the fire-house Frampton.—P.C. Martin arrested him, when he said he had bought 3s. worth of Hobbs, who was Gardener to Mr. Clifford, and the remainder he had picked up. Martin went to Frampton, fitted a piece of lead to another piece on the boathouse, and arrested Hobbs.—The prisoners were bound over to appear at the next Petty Sessions to answer the charge.

Gloucester Journal, 28 December 1861

St Leonards *c.*1823. Following the fire in The Orangery (then called the Green House) at Frampton Court in 1861, Robert Barradell was accused of stealing lead, although he was later discharged. His prison records reveal him to have been 5ft. 6¼in. tall with brown hair, grey eyes, an oval face and sallow complexion. He had a large singular scar between his eyebrows and over his right eye, and moles on his back.

25   VICARAGE LANE – 23 September 1865

William Price

Born *c.*1819, William Price was a sailor from Eastington, married to Mary Ann. The couple's several children attended the National School. However, they had great difficulties in paying their school fees which were 1d. per week per child. The school logbook states: 'Nov. 23rd 1863 – The Prices having paid nothing during the last 6 weeks, Sarah called last week to enquire if they might come and her mother would send the money during the week. They failed as usual but Sarah has called today with 6d. for two of them for 6 weeks.'

This illustrates the hardship that many of the sailors' wives experienced whilst their husbands were away from home. Wages would come into the family infrequently and it must have been extremely hard to struggle through. The school took a fairly lenient view whenever it could, but it was often necessary for children to miss classes for several weeks if there were no money forthcoming.

Caroline Bignell

The caption appears to relate to Caroline Bignell, the wife of Llewellyn, a labourer. Llewellyn

(or Lewin as his name was spelt in the baptism register at Shipton Moyne in 1833) was the eldest of a large family, and it is likely that he followed his younger brother Edwin to Frampton to work on one of the farms. Caroline and Llewellyn had three children christened at Frampton between 1862 and 1867. Their rent was £3 3s. 0d. per annum, which they were unable to pay on time in January 1864 owing to Caroline's ill health.

James Daw

A bricklayer, James Daw was born in Frampton *c.*1807, and married Maria Guy in 1828. They moved to this cottage in Vicarage Lane between 1841 and 1851 with their expanding family. In all they had ten children, although two died whilst very young. It was still relatively common to name a baby after an older brother or sister who had died and their last two daughters, baptised 1852 and 1853 respectively, were named Ellen.

W. Hunt

William Hunt, an agricultural labourer born in Frampton *c.*1835, may have lived in this house for a short while, perhaps after his marriage to Mary Ann. (By 1871 the family had moved to the end of The Street (west), the last cottage before Church Court.) They had 12 children, one of which was making so much noise when the census enumerator called in 1881 he wrote 'Baby, aged 1 month – <u>squalling</u>'. William died in 1910.

26　PARK CORNER – undated

The first two houses depicted are situated at the eastern end of Vicarage Lane and Park Corner can be seen in the background.

Gloucester Journal, 9 January 1864

Fern Cottage

David Long

David Long, a mariner (*c.* 1831–1902) was born in Saul. During the 1860s Ann Elizabeth, David's wife, bore him several children which were all educated, starting school as young as three. It is likely that the Long family were the first occupants of this newly built cottage. Their stay, however, was short, for by 1871 they were living in The Street.

The Ferns

Reuben Charles

Born in Frampton *c.* 1818, Reuben Charles appears to have been the illegitimate son of Elizabeth Charles, a servant. Unable to write, he nevertheless made his way in life, firstly as a mariner and later a barge owner. During the 1860s he was the owner of *Druid* and *Friends* (see Thomas Hobbs, who also owned these boats), and part owner of the trow *Happy-go-Lucky* with William Daw. The vessels sailed between Gloucester, Bridgwater, Cardiff, Bristol and Highbridge, with the average journey taking five days.

Reuben Charles married twice, his first wife Elizabeth dying when 22, after just two years of marriage. Four years later, in 1850, he married Charlotte who lived with him for the following fifty years. Despite his humble beginnings he was the owner of houses and land in The Street by 1879. Reuben Charles died in 1905.

Park Corner

John Phipps

John Phipps (*c.* 1831–1903) was a shepherd from Standish. He married a girl named Mary Ann who came from Sapperton. On the 1861 census they were living at the cottage with no children, probably newly wed. After that, Mary Ann was pregnant almost every alternate year. In 1881 they were still living at Park Corner with seven of their children. One of them, Kate, is pictured in Alan Sutton's *The Severn Vale in Old Photographs*. By 1891 14-year-old Kate was a servant to George Bubb at Nastfield Farm.

Robert Lawrence

Born *c.* 1822, Robert Lawrence was an agricultural labourer. He originated from Saul, and was living at Walk on the 1851 census. After a brief return to Saul he moved with his wife Elizabeth and young family to Park Corner. Elizabeth was still living in the cottage in 1891, Robert having died in 1886.

Both the Lawrence and Phipps families attended the National School, although sometimes rather intermittently. There was a tendency towards truancy particularly from two sons, Job Lawrence and Henry Phipps, who were described in the school logbook as 'old offenders', this being when they were aged nine and seven respectively!

The children at Park Corner would have been called upon to help with the harvest each year, missing school to help in the fields and at home. Although the National School tried to

Frampton Vicarage

coincide the month-long summer holiday with the harvest, the children were often required for much longer periods. Not all of them helped in the fields for the older children were needed at home to look after the babies and prepare food for the family, leaving their mothers free to work. The women and children could earn around 2s. a day harvesting, 1s. 9d. for lifting potatoes and 9d. for weeding and planting. They also cleared the ground of large stones. Families like those living at Park Corner were dependent on this additional source of income.

James Cole

The caption probably refers to James Cole, an agricultural labourer who had been born in Slimbridge *c.*1836. His father Samuel lived at Church Court during the 1860s. James married Elizabeth Mills on 9 September 1866, and the sketch (which is undated) may have been drawn after that date. However, he could have been living in the cottage prior to his marriage. In 1876 Henry James Clifford wrote to his agent, 'James Cole also ought to pay rent, but as he has no regular work and only one arm we must not be too hard on him, but get what we can.' James was nearly blind by the time of the 1881 census and died in 1893.

27   The Vicarage

There is no sketch of The Vicarage in the original book of sketches, and the one shown above is by another (unknown) artist and dates from the 1890s.

Rev. M. W. F. St John

The Rev. Maurice William Ferdinand St John (known as Ferdinand) was vicar of Frampton from 1853 until 1881. Highly regarded in the parish, he was probably the most influential person in the village during the 1860s. Equally at ease with rich and poor, Ferdinand St John worked hard to improve standards in many spheres of village life, often preaching and writing of his ideals. He had been born in Italy *c*.1827, the same year as his Scottish wife, Charlotte. The staff at The Vicarage comprised a cook, housemaid and two ladies' maids, and the St Johns had three children, twins (Henry and Aline) born in 1854, followed by Ferdinand in 1861. Charlotte St John was an enormous support to her husband during his ministry in Frampton. Her musical abilities were appreciated at the National School and church alike, where she played the pianoforte, sang and conducted the choirs. The family took holidays in, amongst other places, Rome, Bournemouth, Scotland and North Wales.

In 1861 the vicar announced his latest idea, a parish magazine, to meet the reading needs of the parish which had increased owing to the advances in local education. Each month the booklet, costing 3d., contained one page of parish news (edited by the vicar) and over twenty pages of stories, religious tracts, prayers and a printed sermon supplied by a source common to many other parish magazines around the country. The locals welcomed the magazine, sending it to family and friends who had left the village, and some had each year's copies bound into a single volume to keep for posterity. There was an emphasis placed on church-related activities, but other deserving causes were liberally mentioned such as concerts in aid of Gloucester Infirmary and the activities of the Mechanics' Institute. It was even noted that the vicar missed two and a half Sundays in 1868 when he broke his arm, having fallen from his horse!

The vicar was actively involved in the day-to-day running of the National School, being its manager and secretary. This involved a diversity of duties such as collecting the school fees each Monday, ordering anything from sewing needles to books and inkstands, testing the children on their reading and standing in for the master when he was ill, or taking the pupils for religious instruction. On hot summer days the girls would have their sewing lessons in The Vicarage's drive where it was shady. (The children were less welcome when they got amongst the vicar's shrubs and damaged them whilst searching for bird's nests, for which they received a warning at school the next day.)

Ferdinand St John was always mindful of catering for the needs of the poor and encouraged them to make some provision for their children's education as well as their old age and infirmity. He was, at various times, chairman and treasurer of the Red Scarf Club, a benefit society which paraded annually through the village wearing their red scarves on Frampton Feast day. In the late 1870s he, together with Thomas Watts (the surgeon and a treasurer of the two Septennial Benefit Clubs), suggested that payments should be deferred until the age of 65 (other than in cases of sickness), thereby effectively advocating an old age pension. The Post Office started its Savings Bank in Frampton in 1864. Although it was an excellent opportunity for people to save even the most modest amounts, some were wary of the venture. To help matters Henry James Clifford and Ferdinand St John opened a Penny Bank for the villagers, investing the money they received from parishioners in the Post Office.

The vicar and local gentry were expected to be generous in their support of good causes and in particular the local schools. The Rev. St John and the Clifford family led by example. In typical Victorian tradition accounts of the various charities regularly appear in the parish magazine giving details of each amount donated.

Throughout his incumbency The Vicarage was host to many visitors as Ferdinand St John sought to broaden his own and the villagers' knowledge on a variety of issues. He welcomed speakers on subjects as diverse as 'Spiritual Destitution in our large Cities' or 'India'. A leading member of the Literary and Mechanics' Institute, he recognised that it did not provide for the

Sept 25/65. John Mills. Vicarage Coachhouse & Stables.   Mrs King   Miss Keating   J. Bignell.

less educated or poorer members of the community, so he established the Tree Coffee House in 1877 as a place for working men to drink tea, coffee and cocoa (at 1d. a cup), read the papers and socialise. Ferdinand St John then set about achieving what was possibly his main objective, the formation of a branch of the Church of England Temperance Society. Critical of those who spent too long and too much in Frampton's five public houses he worked with the Rev. William Lewis, the much respected minister of the Congregational Chapel, who delivered a vigorous address in favour of teetotalism and immediately attracted great support in the village.

Ferdinand St John moved to Kempsford in 1881 and later became Rural Dean of Fairford and a Canon of Gloucester Cathedral. He resided at the Cathedral following his retirement and died there in 1914. In his obituary, the Bishop of Gloucester described Ferdinand St John as having had 'a gentle, sympathetic and peace-loving nature always looking with appreciation at the better side of men'. He is buried in Frampton churchyard with his wife and daughter Aline (who had died in childbirth some years earlier).

28   THE STREET (EAST) AFTER VICARAGE LANE – 25 September 1865
Site of Vicarage Cottage

John Mills

There is little doubt that John Mills was born in Frampton, although the year of his birth is unknown. At his burial in 1880 the parish registers gave his age as 99, but it is possible that he was just over 100, for there was a John Mills baptised in 1779. It is likely that John Mills never knew exactly when he was born as the census entries show him ageing 14 and 17 years during some decades. He and his wife Elizabeth had several children which, after her death, he brought up. John was a bricklayer, although towards the end of his life he worked as a groom.

Vicarage Coachhouse and Stables
Today they are known as The Coach House.

Orchard House

Sarah King

When Sarah's first husband, James Bodnum, died in 1840 she carried on his occupation of beer retailer in order to support herself and their daughter Sarah, then aged seven. In 1847 Sarah (*c*.1794-1879) remarried, becoming Daniel King's third wife. When he died in 1855 she was once again left to run the business alone.

Her daughter Sarah became a much-loved infant teacher at the National School. Many of the children contributed towards gifts when she left to get married in 1867, among which was 'an ornament for the breakfast table'. During the early years of their marriage Sarah (junior) and her husband, Frederick Cowley, a chemist from Cheltenham, lived with Sarah King. The family had a general servant. There is no doubting the strong ties between mother and daughter and it may have been after Sarah King's death in 1879, at the age of 86, that the Cowley family moved away from Frampton. Sarah Cowley was also proud of her father, giving her first two sons three Christian names the last of which in each case was Bodnum.

Isabella Keatinge

Isabella Keatinge (*c*.1799-1865) was the daughter of Colonel Maurice Bagenal St Leger Keatinge, M.P. for Co. Kildare from 1790 until 1802. He was the last of five successive generations of Maurice Keatinges to hold a seat in Parliament and live at Narraghmore, Co. Kildare. His association with Narraghmore ended in 1798 when, during the Rebellion, his newly built mansion house was razed to the ground. The family then travelled, living in Bray, Dublin and Shrewsbury, amongst other places.

In 1790 Maurice Keatinge married Lady Martha, daughter of Anthony Brabazon, the 8th Earl of Meath, who, according to contemporary reports, became 'the delight of the neighbourhood'. They had six daughters, and when Maurice died in Paris in 1835 he left no male heir. Isabella Keatinge is likely to have come to Frampton with her sister, Selina Charlotte St John, who was the mother of the vicar, Maurice William Ferdinand St John.

Providence Cottage

Joseph Bignell

Joseph Bignell was a younger brother of Llewellyn and Edwin Bignell (see sketches 25 and 39) He was baptised in 1846 at Shipton Moyne, the home village of several generations of the Bignell family.

29   THE STREET (EAST) – undated (probably 25 September 1865)

Amberley Cottage

Charles Aldridge

It is likely that the Aldridge family had recently arrived in Frampton when the sketch was drawn, Charles and Ann Aldridge having had their daughter Ambrosine Blanch Fanny (known

as Blanch) baptised in late July 1865. Charles was a waterman and they lived in Amberley Cottage until at least 1871.

Tulip Cottage

John Sallis

John Sallis, born in 1801, was a baker from West Kington in Wiltshire, just south of Acton Turville. He arrived in Frampton sometime before 1836 and later moved to Tulip Cottage. There is confusion regarding the spelling of John's surname (Sallis, Sellis or Sollis), which must have partly arisen from his writing. He signed his name with something of a flourish making the second letter almost indistinct, hence the many variations that appear throughout the records. The couple had one daughter, Ann. John's wife Susannah died in 1869 and he probably remained in the cottage until his death in 1876.

30　BOTTOM OF THE STREET (EAST) – 25 September 1865

Oegrove Farm

This farmhouse was probably built during the early 17th century and the earliest trace of it was as the home of John Dopping in 1628. Known as Doppings House for at least the next two centuries, it was owned in 1645 by Richard Caple (c.1586-1656), a leading puritan who had settled in Pitchcombe after resigning as rector of Eastington in 1633. After various changes of ownership the property formed part of two successive marriage settlements in the 18th century and belonged to the Lockey family from 1745 until 1841 when it was bought by Henry Clifford Clifford whose descendants still own it today. The name Oegrove derives from land called Egrove which formed part of the farm from at least 1727.

John Merrett

John Merrett (*c.*1817-71) farmed Oegrove probably from the death of his father, also John, in 1846. The 1851 census, which describes the property as Highgrove Farm, showed him living with his brother William and two sisters Maria and Margaret. The farm consisted of 32 acres in 1851 but this had increased to 63 by 1861. After John Merrett died in 1871 his sister Margaret and nephew John Thomas Evans Merrett ran the farm for a while.

The newspaper extract may have related to one of the labourers from Oegrove Farm.

Thomas Turner's Farm (*see sketch 31*).

FRAMPTON-ON-SEVERN.—*Death from Burning.*—On Thursday, the 26th ult., a poor cripple, named William Browning, who was bird-keeping in a field called Eygrove, and who had lit a fire for the purpose of warming himself, when it appears the poor fellow's clothes became ignited. His cries were heard by some men in an adjoining field who hastened to his assistance, and with some difficulty extricated him from the fire, his clothes being nearly burnt off. He lingered until Tuesday, when he expired.

Gloucester Journal, 4 April 1863

Site of Denfurlong Cottage

These cottages have been demolished.

Mary Guy

Mary Guy was the widow of John Guy (*c.*1789-1857). They were a very poor family and on the 1851 census John was described as a pauper, agricultural labourer. Having lived in this cottage since before 1841, they paid an annual rent to Henry Clifford Clifford of £2 0s. 0d. which on occasions they found difficult to settle. An example of this was just before John's death when he was bedridden and the couple were receiving parish relief. At that time they owed the equivalent of four years' rent; a situation that remained unchanged for the following

Mary Gengo, Nancy Knight. John Lawrence. Sept 25/65

10 years. Both John and Mary were unable to write and their children do not appear to have gone to school. Illiteracy brought many problems, not least of which was the inability to recall one's age. According to the information Mary gave about herself to the census enumerators she could have been born anytime between 1803 and 1812.

In 1861 three of Mary's children were living with her: Sarah whose occupation was 'servant out of place', and William and Frederick, both agricultural servants. Mary herself was a charwoman and she probably remained in the cottage until her death sometime after the census of 1871.

Ann Knight

Ann (or Nancy) Knight was the widow of William Knight, a seaman. She was born in Hardwicke sometime between 1784 and 1799. The annual rental paid by Ann was £3 1s. 0d.

John Lawrence

John Lawrence, born *c*.1794, gave different details of his birthplace on the various censuses varying between Stonehouse, Frampton and Haresfield. An agricultural labourer, he moved to this cottage between 1841 and 1851, the rental increasing from £4 1s. 0d. to £5 2s. 0d. in 1861 indicating that some sort of extension to the building may have been made at that time. John Lawrence probably dressed in typical labourer's clothes: a round white smock-frock (opening in the front), striped vest, white cotton shirt, cord trousers, light cotton neckerchief and a dark straw hat.

John and his wife Maria had several children and, after she died sometime before 1861, he spent his last years alone in the cottage before dying in 1875.

Sept. 25th   Thomas Turner's Farm.

31   DENFURLONG FARM – 25 September (1865)

Thomas Turner

Born *c*.1793 in Frampton, Thomas Turner married Sarah, the daughter of the previous tenant farmer at Denfurlong, Richard Clarke, in 1822. It was probably upon the death of Richard Clarke in 1855, aged 85, that Thomas Turner began to live at Denfurlong Farm, although he was certainly involved in the running of it from an earlier date. By the time Ann Clarke, Richard's widow, died in 1868 she had lived at the farm for seventy years.

Denfurlong was a dairy farm of 167 acres. In the mid-1860s much of Gloucestershire was affected by the rinderpest, an acute contagious viral disease of cattle which, as the name suggests, had been brought in from the continent. Although the farms in Frampton thankfully escaped rinderpest, the suspension of trading at Gloucester Cattle Market and the high price of meat was felt in the area, special mention of it being made in the parish magazine of January 1866 when the vicar was reflecting on the previous year.

Thomas retired from the farm in 1875, the year his wife died, and lodged with George Workman in The Red House, The Green (west) probably until his death in 1882.

32   CHURCH END HOUSE AND TANHOUSE FARM – 27 September 1865
Site of Tanfield, lane leading to the church

Matilda Evans

Matilda Evans (*c*.1808-91) had married George in 1862, but they kept on this cottage which she had shared with her second husband, Joshua Goulding. She was married to three watermen and outlived them all.

Church End House

This detached house was built in the late 18th century by the Barnard family using their own manufactured bricks. The property was known as Splatt House during the 1860s but by 1887 was called Church End House.

Thomas Bellamy Barnard

Thomas Bellamy Barnard (1811–87) was a brick and tile maker, coal merchant, barge owner and maltster. Unmarried, he lived with two of his spinster sisters Elizabeth and Mary, their father (also Thomas) having owned the property until his own death in 1844. The Barnard family were considered members of Frampton's gentry and Thomas Bellamy was the last in a line of Thomas Barnards. He distinguished himself locally taking on several offices such as Guardian of the Poor, Surveyor of the Highways, Collector of Taxes and Treasurer of the Mechanics' Institute, and ran the Walham Brick Works near Gloucester to which he took his friends from Frampton in 1863.

FRAMPTON-ON-SEVERN. — Thomas Bellamy Barnard, Esq., assisted by other gentlemen, some years ago established a Mechanics' Institute in this village, and from that time to the present Mr. Barnard has continued a staunch supporter of the institution. On Tuesday he gave a treat to as many of the members as chose to partake of his hospitality. Accordingly about 60 members made a passage, per steamer, to Gloucester, when they proceeded to the King's Head, and after partaking of a capital cold collation walked to the brick and tile works of Mr. Barnard, distant about a mile from the city, on the bank of the Severn, where a sumptuous repast awaited them. Altogether it was one of the pleasantest days that many of the members had ever known, and no person seemed to enjoy it more than the worthy "founder of the feast."

Gloucester Chronicle, 4 April 1863

Thomas Bellamy Barnard had opened a new brickworks near Denmark Road, Gloucester that same week and his men were in high spirits, celebrating his success. One of them, his carter James Winter, returned from Gloucester to Walham Brick Works somewhat the worse for liquor and lit a candle on his way to bed in the hay loft where he slept. A fire ensued in the stables and carpenter's shop, signalling a downturn in the luck of Barnard. Although he was insured with Norwich Union, whose engine's prompt attendance prevented the spread of the fire to surrounding buildings, Thomas Bellamy Barnard was declared bankrupt before the end of 1863, and Walham Brick Works was sold early in 1864. Perhaps he had overstretched himself with his latest acquisition at Denmark Road, or maybe the ill health that was mentioned during his bankruptcy hearings had affected the running of the business. Whatever it was, the glory days of the Barnard family were over.

Thomas Bellamy Barnard worshipped at the chapel where he was one of the deacons for many years.

Tanhouse Farm

Matilda Morgan

Matilda Morgan (born *c.*1807) had farmed at Tanhouse Farm from before 1851 until 1879, increasing its size from 20 to 37 acres. A widow from Eastington, she had the help of Thomas Bosworth, a farm labourer some twenty years her junior, for most of the time that she ran the farm. As a haulier she carried goods such as bricks, timber, ballast, sand, manure, coal and lime for local people including Henry Clifford Clifford. Some of these items would have been brought to Frampton via the canal which lay only a hundred yards or so from the farmhouse.

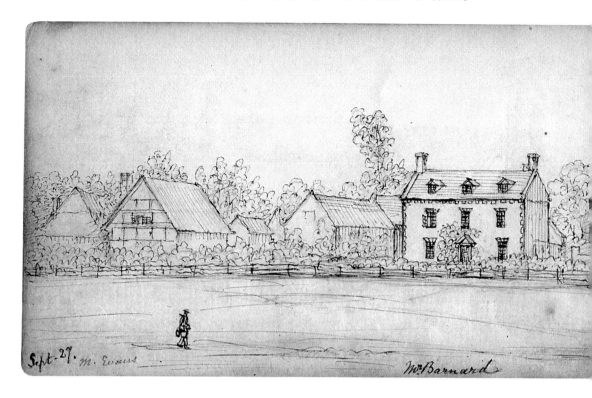

Sept. 27. M. Evans   Mᵣ Barnard

33   FIELD FARM (SPLATT LANE) – 26 September (1865)

These cottages were probably located just to the south of Tanhouse Farm.

George Hazell

George Hazell was born in Hawkesbury Upton (south of Wotton-under-Edge) *c*.1831 and came to Frampton *c*.1851 when, employed as an agricultural carter, he lodged at Park Corner with John and Martha Williams, who were possibly his brother-in-law and sister. A year later George married Martha Browning, the daughter of Henry Browning, a gamekeeper, but their marriage lasted only six years, Martha passing away aged 29, her newly born child having died a few days earlier.

With a young daughter to bring up, George lost no time in finding himself another wife and married Ann Brooks aged 17 in 1859. They had at least twelve more children which put them under a heavy financial strain and, in common with other families in the village, the Hazells were often behind in payment of their school fees. At one stage the schoolmaster sent a bill for the outstanding amount, thereby prompting Mrs. Hazell to remove all her children to the Chapel School (which, incidentally, also charged) to try and avoid paying for a little longer.

George Hazell was variously an agricultural labourer, carter, carrier and hallier (haulier). As a carrier in the late 1880s and early 1890s he made trips every Monday, Wednesday and Saturday to Gloucester, returning the same day. He died in 1903. His children went on to do a variety of jobs from an early age, presumably to help support the large family. These included waterman, telegraph and errand boy, newspaper errand boy, domestic servant and labourer.

Patience Brooks

Patience Brooks (c.1811–85) was the widow of Thomas, a waterman, and the mother of George Hazell's second wife Ann. Thomas Brooks (c.1808–59) married Patience in 1837 after they had both been widowed. Living near the brickyard, at least two of her sons worked there during their teenage years and on the 1861 census Patience's own occupation is described as a 'brickyard woman'. The Brooks were another family to owe Henry Clifford Clifford more than two years' rent (£4 0s. 0d. per annum) over a period of at least a decade.

Sophia Knight and Giles Wilkins

Sophia Knight (c.1804–82) from Whitminster, was the widow of William Knight (c.1798–1864) who had been a bricklayer by trade. In 1841 William and Sophia may well have been living in this cottage whose location was then described as Pill Farm and certainly by 1851 they were in Splatt Lane, their nephew Giles Wilkins, also a bricklayer, living with them. They do not appear to have had any children.

Giles (c.1834–97) was born in Bristol and he married Eliza Ann Wathen from Frampton in 1856. They lived in various homes around the village with their two daughters both of whom subsequently bore several illegitimate children.

FRAMPTON-ON-SEVERN. — ACCIDENT. — On Monday a mason named Giles Wilkins met with an accident from a horse. He had been cutting some stakes to make a stank, when in passing, the animal kicked him severely on the thigh and on the fleshy part of the arm, inflicting rather severe bruises. No bones were broken, and the man is recovering.

Gloucester Chronicle, 7 November 1868

G. Hazle. P. Brooks. S. Knight G. Wilkins. Sept 26.

34 COTTAGES BY THE SPLATT BRIDGE (also known as Salt Marsh Cottages, now Splatt Cottages) – 28 July 1866

John and Harriet Allen

John Allen (*c*.1792-1869) and his wife Harriett had lived here prior to 1851. John (who was born in Saul) and their son Herbert were mariners; Harriett was a sempstress (an old term for seamstress).

GLOUCESTERSHIRE.
Eligible Freehold Investments & Building Land,
At FRAMPTON-UPON-SEVERN,
Near Gloucester.
TO BE SOLD BY AUCTION,
By Mr. *JAMES KARN*,
At the BELL INN, FRAMPTON-UPON-SEVERN, on Thursday, the 21st day of January, 1864, at six o'clock in the afternoon, subject to Conditions, by order of the Assignee of Mr. THOMAS BELLAMY BARNARD, a Bankrupt, in the following Lots :—

Lot 2.—All those Three FREEHOLD COTTAGES or TENEMENTS, and GARDENS attached, adjoining the Gloucester and Berkeley Canal near the Bridge called the Frampton Bridge, in the said parish of Frampton-upon-Severn, and nearly adjoining to the last-mentioned hereditaments, now in the respective occupations of John Allen, James Hooper, and James Winters, at an aggregate rental of £18 per ann. Land Tax, 3s. 6d.

Gloucester Journal, 9 January 1864

James Hooper

James Hooper was a gardener who lived in the village with his wife Jane from midway through the 1860s. Whilst they were in Frampton two of their children died in infancy and Jane Hooper also passed away, aged 36, in 1869. The records of the National School indicate that the family moved to Gloucester early in 1870.

Richard James Winter

Richard James Winter (known as James) was an agricultural labourer from Cirencester born *c*.1827. He was unable to write which may account for his surname sometimes being spelt

July 28./66. Alney. Stinchcombe hill. Slimbridge Spire, Hooper. Winter.   Cottages by the Splat Bridge.

Winters. Richard married Maria, the daughter of George Evans, a local waterman, in 1847. Their first child, Jasper Evans Winter, took his mother's maiden name as his middle name. This was a common occurrence at the beginning of the period where the use of two Christian names instead of one had become increasingly popular. Jasper died just two days after his birth. Several more children followed, among them two called Richard James Winter, the first of whom only lived for 11 months.

Many children in the village started work at an early age, but the entries in the National School logbook that follow show just how young some of them were:

> Dec. 1st 1862 – We also readmitted W. Winter who has been absent for the last three years at work.
> Dec. 8th 1862 – W. Winter after coming nearly a whole week has again left to go to work. I am told to be at Mr. Cliffords. He is 9 years old.

Most farmers during the 1860s hired their employees on an annual basis, often at the local 'Mop' Fairs. Prospective workers stood in the market place with some symbol of their trade to indicate the employment they were seeking; thatchers with a fragment of woven straw in their hats and shepherds with sheep crooks in their hands, for example. In a village such as Frampton the arrangements for hiring may have been accomplished on a more individual basis. Whatever the terms of James Winter's employment with Edward Watts at Parks Farm in 1860, they do not appear to have been fully understood by those involved (see newspaper cutting overleaf).

Richard James Winter moved from Splatt shortly after the sketch was drawn and lived for many years in Vicarage Lane. He died in 1894 and Maria, his wife, in 1900.

Gloucester Journal, 30 March 1861

35 SPLATT BRIDGE HOUSE – 13 October 1865

Originally the bridgekeeper's house at Splatt Bridge on the Gloucester and Berkeley Canal, this property was built in the early 19th century and was possibly designed by Robert Mylne, the first principal engineer to the Gloucester and Berkeley Canal Company. There are several other similar houses along the canal, which was opened in 1827.

Thomas Rea

Thomas Rea (born *c.*1797) came from Frampton and married his first wife Mary in 1818. She bore him several children before her death in 1840 at the age of 47. At that time Thomas was a labourer living in one of the cottages (since demolished) at the bottom of The Street. By 1851 he had moved to the bridgekeeper's house at Splatt Bridge where he remained for the

Splat Bridge   T. Rea

rest of his life. Neither he nor either of his wives could write and the children seem to have had a mixed education for some were literate and some not. It also appears that they left home to find a living as soon as they were able, several of them initially as domestic servants. One son, Charles, then aged ten, was noted in the school logbook: 'Nov. 24th 1862 – Commence the week with the return of C. Rea after being absent all summer keeping sheep etc.'

When Thomas and his second wife Betsy both died in 1874, their son Charles took over the job of bridgekeeper and with it the little house beside the canal. He had always lived at home, the youngest in the family, and latterly he had probably helped his father.

The volume of traffic on the canal varied from day to day depending on the weather and time of year. Each day steamers (*The Lapwing* and *The Wave*) made regular trips along the length of the canal, and on Monday, Wednesday and Saturday 'market boats' took goods and passengers to Gloucester, leaving Frampton at 8.30a.m. and returning from Gloucester at 4.30p.m. Larger boats, of which there could be any number depending on the tides and time of year, required the bridges to be opened, whilst the smaller barges sailed under.

The canal was used for leisure activities including swimming, fishing and skating. Occasionally accidents befell swimmers that were sometimes fatal and these were widely reported in the weekly newspapers, the *Gloucester Journal* and *Gloucester Chronicle*, both of which covered events all over the county and also gave worldwide news. Many varieties of fish lived in the canal and one particular fishing party in 1868 reported catching '35 jack, two large carp, several large and very fine eels and almost any quantity of white fish'. In the winter sometimes the canal froze over thereby allowing skaters to have some fun. (The schoolchildren also enjoyed sliding on the village ponds on the green.)

36 COTTAGE IN POUND LANE – undated

This picture is one of only two watercolours in the sketchbook, the other being the rear of Frampton Court. The cottage was situated alongside the track to the church, which was known as Pound Lane or Church Lane, for it led to the village pound. The site of the cottage is now occupied by the church car park.

Henry Perks

Henry Perks was born in Frampton *c.*1807. A bricklayer by trade, he married Jane Click from Burlescombe in Devon in 1837. A keen gardener, Henry rented some ground for one shilling from Henry Clifford Clifford where he grew vegetables and fruit, winning several prizes for apples, redcurrants, potatoes and herbs at the annual shows during the mid-1860s.

Henry Perks died in 1881, having outlived his wife by four years. He left this cottage and a personal estate of £90 9s. 1d. to his niece Emily Harris who was then approached by Henry James Clifford and later his son Henry Francis Clifford regarding ownership of the building. The Cliffords maintained that it had been built by a squatter on their land and that they were therefore the rightful owners. In 1902 Emily Harris offered the cottage to Henry Francis Clifford for a sum of £45.

37 ST MARY'S CHURCH – 20 September 1865

St Mary's Church was consecrated in 1315 and the building dates mainly to the 14th century with some 15th century additions. The oak pulpit bears the names of the churchwardens at the time of its erection in 1622 and the tower was rebuilt in c.1734. The oldest feature in the church is the font, one of six similar Romanesque lead fonts surviving in Gloucestershire. Opinion differs regarding the age of these fonts which

have been variously described as Saxon, Norman (copying the Saxon style in parts, but not earlier than 1100) or a product of the Anglo-Norman school (possibly working locally) in the third quarter of the 12th century.

The church of the 1860s was a growing one. The 19th century witnessed many developments in the work and concerns of all the various denominations throughout the country, and in Frampton the situation was no different. The village finally saw the dismissal of the Rev. James Hartley Dunsford in 1847. Dunsford had been so typical of many late 18th-/early 19th-century clergymen; he very rarely attended the church at Frampton leaving a succession of curates to carry out his clerical duties and lead the services. During the whole of his incumbency (1813-47) he took only 15 burial services, and six of those were in the two months prior to his institution as vicar. A pluralist, the Rev. Dunsford simultaneously held the stipendiary curacy of Slimbridge (where he lived), the rectory of Fretherne and the vicarage of Frampton.

The Rev. George Chute, who succeeded Dunsford, took his duties more seriously and evening services began to be held in Fromebridge. An Irishman with a young family, the Rev. Chute oversaw the church's restoration in 1850-2 and stayed until 1853 when the Rev. Maurice William Ferdinand St John became Frampton's vicar. His arrival marked the beginning of a new era in the history of the church in Frampton, although the changes he introduced were made gradually and usually with the parishioners' consent. By this time the Church of England clergy had generally become more professional and responsible, and saw their rôle as leaders not just within their church but amongst the local community where they could exert great influence.

In Frampton the church and chapel existed quite happily alongside one another, with each respecting the other's differences. The replacement of the old metrical psalms at St Mary's with

the new *Hymns Ancient and Modern* in 1864 was well received and the hymnbooks were sold by John Sumner at his stationery shop in the village.

In 1866, as a further improvement to the music, a new organ was erected by J. W. Walker & Sons of London at a cost of £209 5s. 6d., which was borne by an anonymous benefactor. A report in the parish magazine tells of how it was played by Hubert Parry, then aged 18, the talented son of Mr. Thomas Gambier Parry of Highnam Court. (Sir Hubert Parry, later to compose the hymn tune *Jerusalem*, became a fine English church musician, and was a frequent visitor to Frampton in his early days. His mother was also a regular soloist at concerts in the village.)

There was a great choral tradition built up in Frampton during the 1860s, assisted no doubt by the vicar's wife who was an accomplished musician. The church choir often gave concerts in the church or the schoolroom and on All Saints' Day in 1865 the church choirs of Frampton, Framilode, Hardwicke and Standish joined together to form the Frampton Choral Union. Their first concert in April 1866 drew together 118 singers of whom 39 came from Frampton. The Union prided itself on attracting members from all classes, cottager and squire alike.

Early each January the young choristers were treated to tea at the National School, where the Christmas tree was laden with presents for every child, generously given by members of the Watts family. Surplices were not provided for the choristers until 1876, at which time their behaviour and punctuality improved with 'no boy being admitted to the stalls after the commencement of the service'. With their clothes covered by the surplices the choristers became classless, much to the delight of the vicar.

The older children of the National School attended church almost every day throughout Lent and on Saints' Days, Ascension Day and other important dates in the church's calendar.

2 house behind.   _James Guy._   _Giles Frape. Clerk._

At about 11 o'clock they would walk to church for a service which lasted about 30-40 minutes. On Ascension Day in 1868 one of the boys, C. Aldridge, struck some matches in church thereby causing a suffocating smell to spread all over the building, no doubt much to the amusement of the other children. His glory was short-lived for the vicar noticed and complained to his parents about him.

In 1867 the churchyard was extended, and a year later the pulpit was moved and the height of the reading desk reduced to enable the congregation to hear more clearly. Also in 1867 the parish received a set of solid gold communion plate following a generous bequest of £1,000 from the late Miss Ann Wicks who had died almost thirty years earlier. The vicar and churchwardens were concerned for its safety and were warned by the police not to keep it in the church for burglaries were rife in the neighbourhood. It was removed to Gloucester, sold and eventually replaced by a communion set of silver-gilt, the balance of monies being used towards the restoration of the church in 1870.

Throughout the decade Ferdinand St John had widened the knowledge of his parishioners by inviting a series of preachers to address them. The subjects varied enormously and were often concerned with missions both abroad and in England. Much encouragement was given from the pulpit for local charitable acts and the parishioners were given advice on how to improve themselves and their lot in life.

38   CHURCH COURT – 28 September 1865

Church End Cottage
This small, detached cottage was probably built during the late 17th century.

Ann (Hannah) Wright

Ann (or Hannah) Wright was the wife of William Knight-Wright, a waterman. The couple lived in Church Court, most probably at Church End Cottage, for all their married lives together with their several children. Ann (*c*.1816-99) was still in the cottage in 1891, William having died some three years earlier. Their annual rent was £3 10s. 0d.

Samuel Cole (or Coole)

Samuel's surname was variously recorded as Cole or Coole. Born in Standish, Samuel (*c*.1810-93) and his wife Elizabeth had nine children. The family moved to Church End Cottage sometime before 1861 having previously lived in The Street. He was primarily a labourer who, for a short while, also turned his hand to being a dealer in marine stores.

Church Court

William Guy

Another longstanding inhabitant of Church Court, William Guy (*c*.1791-1872) had lived mainly in Churchside Cottage having married Hannah Lambourn in 1814 in her home village of Berkeley. When the sketch was drawn the couple had recently swapped cottages with their son James (mentioned below). One of their daughters was Ann (Hannah) Wright of Church End Cottage (see above). Along with many of the Guy family members William was a waterman.

William Woodward

William Woodward (born *c*.1832), an agricultural labourer from Stonehouse, married Frampton-born Ann Guy in 1857. Neither was able to write. Later their children attended the National School and, like so many families in Frampton, William and Ann would have depended on their offspring to read any important documents for them. The children may also have read aloud to their parents from magazines and newspapers if the family could afford them.

Churchside Cottage
Formerly the outbuildings to Church Court Cottage (see below), Churchside Cottage dates to around the late 17th or early 18th century.

James Guy

James Guy was a mariner born in Frampton *c*.1816, the son of William (see above). He was unable to write when he married a local girl, Hannah Rea, in 1838, although she was able to sign her name. James being away from home in 1861, Hannah was left to complete her family's details for the census enumerator. She had certain difficulties with one child aged four, giving its relationship as both son and daughter and then finally son, before calling it Mary which was then crossed out! That child, James Guy (junior) was to fare little better at school; his first appearance in the National School logbook aged six recorded his payment of 6d. for a broken window. During James junior's school career he suffered the indignity of being downgraded to a lower class, and his inability to read and write properly caused the master much concern.

In 1891, still living in Church Court, James Guy was a widower with his widowed daughter Ellen looking after him. He died five days before the beginning of the new century.

Church Court Cottage

Originally a farmhouse, Church Court Cottage was probably built in the early 17th century.

Giles Frape

Born in Frampton *c.*1795 Giles Frape was a bricklayer by trade. He married Mary Powell from Horsley in 1820 and by the end of 1822 he had taken over the job of parish clerk from Giles Griffin who had died in September of that year. Witnessing many of the marriages during the next twenty years, his signature appears often in the registers, particularly when the bride, groom and witnesses were all unable to write. As the population became more literate witnesses were able to sign for themselves, although one suspects that Giles Frape was still in attendance at the ceremonies. As sexton he acted as caretaker of the church and churchyard and would probably have been the gravedigger too. The post of parish clerk was, in those days, one of great importance and it is therefore no surprise to find his house very near to the church and his status noted on the sketch. His wife was employed as pew opener earning a guinea a year in 1848.

Giles and Mary Frape appear to have been a caring couple although they may have been less than pleased when their eldest daughter Ann gave birth to two illegitimate children. Nevertheless these two youngsters were brought up in the Frape family home which was often full of children and grandchildren. All the children were educated and some went on to teach at the National School, notably their youngest daughter Mary Elwina who was sewing mistress from 1868 to *c.*1885. Giles found time to tend his garden and won many prizes in the local shows in the 1860s for fruit, vegetables and flowers. He must have been particularly delighted that two of his daughters chose to marry gardeners.

In 1871 a company of bell ringers was formed (although the bells had been rung previously), with practice each Wednesday. It became a tradition to ring out the old year and ring in the new and in 1876 the parish magazine tells how the able set of ringers were led by the 'marvellous energy of their old leader and teacher, the parish clerk, who is keener than any, although he has now passed his 80th birthday'.

Giles Frape was active to the last. An accidental fall from the canal bridge into the water in 1880 caused a severe shock to his system, and although he was immediately rescued and taken to his home, he died a few hours later. According to the Rev. Ferdinand St John, Giles Frape 'had earned the respect and goodwill of all parishioners, and of late he had been waiting in faith and patience for his Master's summons'. He was 85 when he died.

The office of parish clerk and sexton was filled by William Gleed, husband of Mary Elwina Frape (see above). The Gleeds had married several years before, and with their own son had been living in Church Court Cottage. It is likely that Giles Frape had prepared his son-in-law for the duties that he now took on and they may well have been working together for some while, for the vicar's appointment of William Gleed was immediate.

39 MRS. FRENCH'S FARMYARD, CHURCH END – 29 September 1865

This relates to Church Farm, then in the occupation of Jane French (see sketch 45). Until the early 1840s the farmhouse was situated here. Church End is likely to have formed the original part of the village and would have comprised more dwellings many centuries ago. The building on the left of the sketch is variously reputed to be part of the former manor house or the priest's house, and dates to the early 16th century. The

large barn (not shown on the sketch) is thought to have been rebuilt immediately after a violent storm in 1688 using fabric from the late 16th and early 17th centuries.

Edwin Bignell

This property has been demolished.
Edwin Bignell, a carter, was born *c.*1835 in Shipton Moyne, Wiltshire, the brother of Llewellyn and Joseph (see sketches 25 and 28). His wife Jane came from Ashton Keynes and was ten years his senior. They arrived in Frampton at the beginning of the 1860s and at the time of the sketch had a very young family.

40   HOUSE JUST BEFORE CHURCH COURT, CHURCH END – 2 October 1865

This property has been demolished.

Charles Roberts

Charles Roberts (*c.*1805-70) was originally a waterman, although he later became an agricultural labourer. Born in Frampton, he married twice, on both occasions to a woman called Hannah, and had five children.

David Aldridge and Thomas Rea

David Aldridge was born *c.*1793 in Standish and married Kitty Kemmett of Frampton in 1816. He was a labourer, unable to write, but a good gardener. The couple appear to have moved to this cottage during the 1840s with their several children and paid 4 guineas rent to Henry Clifford Clifford.

David Aldridge had been friends with Thomas Rea (see sketch 35) for a long time and witnessed Thomas' marriage in 1818. It is no surprise to find David's daughter Ann married to Thomas' son, also called Thomas (*c*.1833-87). The young couple were living with David Aldridge, by then a widower, at the time of the sketch. Ann was engaged as infant teacher at the National School for a month in 1869 whilst Miss Evans was away ill. David Aldridge died in 1875 of 'old age and general decay'.

41 THE STREET (WEST) – 26 September 1865

Combe Cottage

William Hawkins

William Hawkins (*c*.1830-80) was a mariner who, on his way home from work one day, became involved in an incident (see right).

Born in Frampton, he married Harriet Aldridge in 1852 and they had four children. As master of various vessels he plied the Gloucester and Berkeley Canal and would have spent a large part of the year away from home. At the age of nine his son, also William, had a spell working at the brickyard situated between the church in Frampton and the canal. Judging by the school logbook entries, he spent his summers working and his winters at school.

was fined in the penalty of 10*l*. or three months' imprisonment.

WHITMINSTER PETTY SESSIONS, *Feb.* 23.—Before H. H. Wilton and N. H. Marling, Esqrs. and the Rev. T. Peters.— *William Hawkins*, a waterman, of Frampton, was charged with assaulting, on the 18th inst. Mr. John Smith, of Overton Farm, in the parish of Arlingham. It appeared that Mr. Smith and his men were planting wheat in a field on his farm, when the defendant came over a wall, and walked on the newly-sown corn, where there was no path. Complainant remonstrated with him, and wished him to return. Defendant said it was his nearest way home, and he would go. Complainant held his walking-stick over his head, and tried to stop him, when defendant took hold of the stick, and they struggled together for some time. There being cross-summonses, the Bench decided on hearing both sides, and Hawkins then gave his version of the affair. The Bench said they thought both parties were to blame. Mr. Smith had no right to hold the stick over Hawkins's head, which amounted to an assault, and Hawkins had no right trespassing on Mr. Smith's land, and they should convict them both. Hawkins was fined 2*s*. 6*d*. and 17*s*. costs; and Smith, 1*s*. and 11*s*. costs.—*Elizabeth Barrow*, a little girl, of Whitminster, was charged with breaking down and destroying a hedge belong-

Gloucester Journal, 25 February 1860

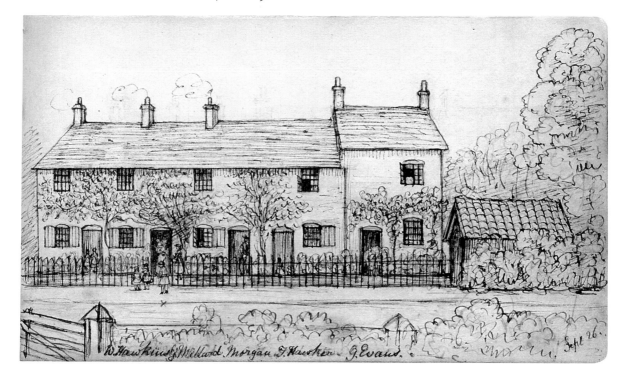

W. Hawkins. Millard. Morgan. T. Hawker. G. Evans.

School Row

Giles Millard

Giles Millard (c.1835–1914) was a gardener and farm labourer, born in Frocester. He married Hannah who was about four years older than him. The Millards rented various properties around the village, perhaps seeking larger accommodation as their family grew in size. Giles had five children and a stepdaughter. An outbreak of smallpox in their household in 1872 prompted many in the village to be vaccinated.

From time to time the vicar arranged for special lectures to be given at the National School, and it is likely that the children were particularly interested in one in 1868 on Electricity, for which an admission charge of 1d. was made. The Millards would also have remembered 'Gun Powder Plot day' later in the year. The master of the school gave all the children a timely warning against the use of gunpowder, the pupil teacher (William Hobbs) having had his face burnt at school with the substance just a month earlier.

Morgan

This cottage was most probably occupied by Henry and Ann Morgan and their two young daughters. An agricultural labourer born in Arlingham c.1829, Henry was not closely connected with the other Morgan families in Frampton.

Thomas Hawker

Thomas Hawker (1835–1907), a brickmaker and layer, was the son of Dorcas Hawker who lived at The Old Thatch just a few doors further up The Street. Following his marriage to Ann

Dorcas Hawker.   Oct 2.

Maria Goulding in 1859, he had a total of nine children, five of whom were baptised during the 1860s. Thomas was later employed as a foreman on a steam dredger.

George Evans

George Evans (*c.*1817-76), like his father a waterman, had lived at 1 School Row from sometime before 1851 with his first wife Elizabeth. Although she died in 1862 and he married Matilda Goulding, a widow, later that year, George and Matilda appear in separate dwellings on the sketches, Matilda having retained her former marital home near the church. By 1871 they were both living at Matilda's cottage.

The True Heart

Mark Cook

This beerhouse is not shown on the sketches, but certainly by the mid-1860s (and perhaps earlier) Mark Cook (*c.*1820-93) and his wife Hannah were running the business. Mark was also a waterman. They do not appear to have had any children.

42 THE OLD THATCH – 2 October 1865

This detached cottage was formerly the farmhouse for the Yew Tree Farm estate. Dating to the late 15th or early 16th century, it was said also to have been used as a place of worship by the nonconformists after the Act of Uniformity in 1662. The Old Thatch was sold in 1838 for £90 by Henry Clifford Clifford.

Dorcas Hawker

When Dorcas Hawker (*c.*1798-1870) was widowed in 1844 she was left with the task of bringing up 11 children. Mary, the eldest of these, died just two years after her father, and the family must have been hit particularly hard.

Thomas Hawker, Dorcas' husband, had been a hallier (haulier) and, following his death, Dorcas carried on the business. Dorcas is probably pictured outside her cottage on the sketch, wearing her apron. After she died Thomas, one of her sons, came to live in The Old Thatch (see sketch 41).

43   THE STREET (WEST) – 2 October 1865
Ferndale

James Hawkins

James Hawkins (*c.*1795-1873) was a mariner born in Frampton. He married Elizabeth Woodman in 1823 and, as was often the case in those days, the first two of their six children took their parents' names, Elizabeth and James.

The New Inn (now Roseleigh)

Cornelius Carter

Cornelius Carter (*c.*1821-98) was a mariner and beer seller, born in Arlingham. When Cornelius was away at sea he left his wife Elizabeth to run the beerhouse. At the end of 1870 his New

Year's Eve celebration went on beyond time and he was fined 2s. 6d. with 8s. expenses by the magistrates who by then met in the specially built court room adjoining the police station at Whitminster (having until 1867 presided in a small room in the *Whitminster Inn*).

44   THE STREET (WEST) – 3 October 1865

The Laurels

Thomas Morgan

The Laurels had been the Morgan family's home from before 1838 when John Morgan, the tenant, bought the house, workshop, outbuildings and garden from Henry Clifford Clifford for £156. John Morgan, head of the family of bricklayers and builders, died in 1861. Thomas (*c.*1823-95), one of his sons, lived in the property all his life. Thomas married three times and is buried with his first and third wives in the churchyard. His second wife, Mary Ann, was the widow of Charles Evans, a schoolmaster, with whom she is buried.

The following referred to an extension built at the National School:

FRAMPTON-ON-SEVERN.—On Thursday, the 28th inst., a tea meeting was held at the National School, to which the choir and the workmen employed in the construction of the school were invited. After tea the Vicar made an appropriate address, congratulating the builder, Mr. Thomas Morgan, on the successful completion of the building, which, he was happy to say, was already paid for. The choir then performed several pieces of sacred and secular music in capital style, particularly the magnificent choruses from the *Messiah*— "The glory of the Lord shall be revealed," and "Who is the king of glory?"—which elicited warm applause. The entertainment closed with the National Anthem. In connection with the late concert and bazaar, we may state that the sum of 63*l.* 1*s.* 8*d.* was realized by the former, and 19*l.* 5*s.* by the latter.

Gloucester Journal, 6 September 1862

Thomas Morgan was also the Registrar of Births and Deaths for Frampton from 1875 until his death. In his capacity as registrar he oversaw the 1881 and 1891 censuses. He was also an agent of the Norwich Union Fire Insurance Society.

Cottage immediately south of The Summer House

This cottage has been demolished.

John Alder

John Alder's mother Mary was unmarried when she gave birth to John and, in order to receive financial help with his upbringing from the Overseers of the Poor of Frampton it was necessary to have him baptised. This happened on 2 January 1803. On 31 May that same year the following appeared against the baptism entry of her daughter: 'Sarah, base daughter of Mary Alder. This child is several years older than her brother John baptised January, but by

neglect of her mother had not been baptised that I could learn'. Both children then became a charge on the parish. At the age of seven John Alder was sent to work, possibly on the farm then run by George Webb who was churchwarden at the time. Later he was given 'a new Breech and a Frock Smock' by the parish and in 1816 he was apprenticed to Henry Workman on a local farm until the age of 18.

In 1829 he married Elizabeth Heiron who may have been the sister of Richard Heiron (see sketch 21). Unusually for a labourer and tile maker, John Alder owned two thatched cottages with gardens, which he bought for £130 in 1838 when Henry Clifford Clifford sold part of his estate in Frampton. At this time Richard Heiron bought the neighbouring property, The Summer House, so perhaps Elizabeth and Richard had come into some money, for it is unlikely that John Alder had any savings. Elizabeth, a tailoress, predeceased him by eight years. Their only child had been a son Jasper, who had died aged 10 weeks.

With no children to leave his cottages to, John Alder made over the two properties to the vicar of the parish on the understanding that they should be used for the permanent benefit of the National School. He wanted the proceeds of their sale to be used to build a new house for the master so as to save the expense of house rent for the future. John Alder could neither read nor write, but was anxious that the children of the village should have the advantages of a schooling that he had never had.

John Alder was probably unaware that his generous bequest would take many years to put into action. The problems were twofold. Firstly, John Alder died in 1874 owing £26 and the cottages needed some repair work before they could be sold. The people of Frampton rallied round; at least two fêtes were held (in 1876 and 1879) in the grounds of Frampton Court to raise money, and collections were made in church towards the project. The second difficulty,

John Alder   R. Hieron   A. Ayland

linked to the first, was that the value of the two cottages was not enough to fund the building of a new schoolmaster's house.

Eventually, a parcel of land was purchased on very advantageous terms following the sale of John Alder's cottages and a new schoolmaster's house was built. Today this property is still called 'Old School House' and can be found opposite the National School in The Street.

Richard Heiron (see sketch 21); Ann Ayland (see sketch 22)

45   THE STREET – 4 October 1865

Church Farm
Built in the early to mid-18th century, this became the new farmhouse for Church Farm between 1841 and 1851. The original farmhouse was situated behind the old barn near Church End (see sketch 39).

Jane French

Jane French first farmed at Townfield Farm with her husband Thomas, where at the time of the 1841 census they had five small children. By 1851 four more infants had been born, Thomas had died, and Jane and her children (the oldest of whom was 17) had moved to Church Farm. She was 43 and employing five labourers.

Money was extremely tight on the farm and Jane French came very close to losing the tenancy in 1859. She struggled to find enough money to pay the rent of £371 5s. 8d. each year. The sale of her wheat did not realise sufficient funds for the outstanding rent of £60 until some cows and heifers were sold at Gloucester market two months later. Henry Clifford

Clifford and his agent from Dursley were compassionate men and they gave her another chance, hoping that her brothers might see her through the crisis, which they evidently did.

Gloucester Journal, 30 November 1861

A year earlier one of Jane French's employees was taking a horse and empty cart down The Street in Frampton when the horse took fright and the poor lad was thrown, his head coming into contact with one of the wheels. The boy was killed instantly and his body was removed to the church porch to await the coroner's inquest.

The French family worshipped at the chapel where the daughters assisted with the catering arrangements at the frequent 'Tea Meetings'. In 1871 the farm was run by Jane's son, Samuel Phelps French, and his wife.

Heart of Oak

The sketch unfortunately does not clearly show Heart of Oak, which was built c. 1754. (It is to the right of Church Farm, behind the trees.) Beer had been retailed from the premises at least as early as 1776 when on the Land Tax Assessment it was simply referred to as 'The Inn'.

J. Evans. E. Morgan. S. Wools. J. Burr. Allen

William Lodge

William Lodge (*c.*1781–1868), a cabinet maker, had lived in the house from sometime before 1841 with both his first and second wives Hannah and Mary Ann. When Mary Ann died he took a housekeeper, Mary Rowles from Arlingham, who continued to live there and run the business after William's death.

It is believed that William Lodge was the last of the Frampton-born Frampton Volunteers to die. The Frampton Volunteers were a local militia set up in 1798 by the then squire Nathaniel Winchcombe to fight in the defence of their country up to a radius of 8 miles from Frampton 'but no more'. The government had reviewed the country's defences in the light of the Napoleonic Wars, and Pitt's Volunteer Defence Act, or Volunteer Corps Act of 1794, was the first legislative attempt to requisition the manpower of England for military service by offering (for

TO BE SOLD BY AUCTION,
By JAMES KARN,
At the Bell Inn, Frampton, at Five o'clock on Monday, the 8th day of March, 1869,—

ALL those extensive PREMISES (situate in the centre of the village of Frampton), known as the HEART OF OAK BEERHOUSE, with large Garden, Yard, and Stable, capital Malthouse, and other convenient Buildings, together with a thriving and well-planted Orchard, now in its prime.

Further particulars will be given in future papers and handbills. For a view apply to the Tenant; and for further particulars to the Auctioneer, Severn Cottage, Newnham.

Gloucester Journal, 6 March 1869

the first time) the choice of service in the Militia or in the Volunteer Corps. The 1798 Defence of the Realm Act stirred the peaceful folk of Frampton and the surrounding villages of Eastington, Stonehouse, Whitminster and Arlingham into establishing the Frampton Volunteers.

Nathaniel Winchcombe (who later changed his name to Clifford and was the father of

John Guy

Henry Clifford Clifford) organised a Resolution for the 110 volunteers to sign on 30 April 1798. It stated that the Corps expected the government to supply muskets and bayonets, whilst they themselves would provide uniforms and whatever else they would need. The uniforms detailed in the Order Book sound rather splendid: round hat with cockade and scarlet feather; scarlet jacket faced with blue, lined and edged white, turnbacks blue; white waistcoat and breeches; gilt button with 'F.V.' surmounted by a crown; white cotton stockings, black velvet hose, half gaiters of black cloth. Members of the Corps band wore almost identical uniforms, the only difference being their jackets which were blue with scarlet facings, lined and edged in white with scarlet turnbacks. William Lodge was a member of the band playing the fife and drum.

There was some delay in sending arms to the Corps, and ammunition was far from plentiful. At first they were allowed just 20 blanks and 6 shots per man for a year's firing practice. Members of the Corps were expected to attend four hours training a week with absence resulting in a fine of 6d. per hour. There were fines for attending parades with dirty equipment (2s. 6d.) or turning out without one's hair combed and properly cut, or shoes not blacked (2s. 6d.). Money from fines was used to fund more instruments. Failure to attend if called to active service would have resulted in a fine of £50 for commissioned officers, £30 for non-commissioned officers and £20 for the rest.

Luckily the Frampton Volunteers did not see any hostile action and the Corps only lasted a few years but the members earned themselves a respected place in the history of the village and are still spoken of with affection today.

John Evans, Edward Morgan, Samuel Wooles, John Burr and Amelia Allen (see sketch 19).

46 WHITTLES LANE – 4 October 1865

Tulip Cottage

Tulip Cottage was built in the late 16th or early 17th century.

John Guy

John Guy was a builder, born in Frampton *c*.1785. He may have married twice; to Rebecca with whom he had several children, and later Elizabeth, a dressmaker from Cranham. The notice of his death in the *Gloucester Journal* reads: 'April 1st 1869 – at Frampton on Severn, Mr. John Guy, aged 84 years. The deceased was for many years employed as a mason to the late H.C. Clifford Esq., and was respected by him and the parishioners generally'.

The Old School House

The property was used during the 19th century as a school, but the dates are uncertain. It was owned by a schoolmaster in 1815, and was referred to as The School House in the Register of Electors of 1881. At that time the location was known as School Lane.

Ann Whittle

Ann Whittle (*c*.1800-78) was the widow of Thomas Whittle, who had bought the property for £340 in 1852. He died in 1856 leaving the house to his widow, to pass on her death to their only son Solomon.

    The 1861 census described Ann as a 'fundholder and proprietor of houses'. She had been born in Whitminster and her son in Longney. Both Ann and Solomon Whittle were noted in the local directories as being among the gentry of the parish and he was an Assistant Overseer of the Poor.

W Hitchings. a Burman. Bond J Draper. W Wotton, Har

47   THE STREET (WEST) – undated (probably October 1865)

Cardiff House

Nathaniel Stockham

Born in Minchinhampton, Nathaniel Stockham (*c.*1834-1903) moved to Frampton a little before the 1861 census, living first in Cardiff House. He was a shopkeeper selling groceries, glass and china, and drapery. The positions of the old shop windows are still visible on the property today. Married to Annie (from Dursley), Nathaniel only spent a short while at Cardiff House before moving to The Green (west) where he opened a larger shop just north of the lane leading to the chapel.

His two daughters, Lizzie and Carrie, helped in the shop and Lizzie is said to have been the first lady in Frampton to ride a bicycle. A post office was incorporated into the shop on The Green and Lizzie took over the running of this and the shop when her father retired. She in turn retired towards the end of the Second World War when she was in her seventies.

Beehive Cottage
Beehive Cottage and Falfield Cottage are said to have been formerly one house which was later enlarged into two dwellings. Reputedly they were rebuilt in 1560 after a storm.

Walter Hitchings

Walter Hitchings (*c.*1829-91), a Frampton-born carpenter and joiner, was the son of John Hitchings, a joiner from Pembrokeshire. He married Mary Cordelia, the daughter of William Dowdeswell Orchard, and they moved to Beehive Cottage *c.*1854 from Saul. The Hitchings had at least twelve children and probably stayed in Beehive Cottage until 1872.

It was as secretary of the Frampton on Severn Friendly Society that Walter Hitchings worked indefatigably for the villagers in the early 1860s. With the vicar as chairman and later treasurer, the society was known locally as the Red Scarf Club on account of the crimson scarves worn during their annual meeting. Starting at the *Bell Inn* members processed behind a local band (Saul Brass Band and Gloucester Wagon Works Band took part in 1861 and 1864 respectively) along the length of The Green, down The Street and on to St Mary's Church where a service was held. The purpose of the society was to assist members to provide for themselves and their families in times of sickness and old age, and the vicar lost no time in reminding those gathered of these duties when he preached his annual sermon.

Once the service was ended the procession retraced its steps to the *Bell* where a sumptuous meal was served in 'host Karn's usual style'. Numbering 120 in the mid–1860s, the society grew in membership to 170 a decade later, when the vicar was advocating an old age pension from the age of 65.

Falfield Cottage

Ann Burman

Ann (*c.*1797-1883), widowed with a young son, married John Burman in Hempstead in 1826. The family was very poor and by late 1829 had become a financial drain on the parish. The Overseers sought to apply to the Petty Sessional Court at Whitminster to obtain an Order of Removal of the family back to John Burman's home parish of Charwelton, Northamptonshire. This was not an uncommon occurrence for even though Ann had been born in Frampton she automatically took the settlement of her husband upon their marriage. Somehow they managed to survive the crisis and stayed in Frampton; perhaps the Overseers relented or the Burmans enjoyed better times. The couple and their large family had lived in one half of Greycroft (see below) for a while, but around the time of John's death in 1846 moved next door to Falfield Cottage. Ann was a laundress who took in not only washing but also lodgers.

Greycroft

A small, detached cottage, the oldest part (towards the north) of Greycroft may have been built in the 15th century. The building was extended or refaced on the southern side probably in the 17th century. Throughout the 19th century Greycroft remained as two properties, each consisting of one living room downstairs and one bedroom upstairs. The accommodation was typical of a small cottage and many of the families in Frampton would have lived in a similar way to the occupants of Greycroft.

Each front door opened straight into the living area, the room measuring around 17½ft. by 16½ft. A large fireplace enabled the family to cook and keep warm when they could afford the fuel. The small windows allowed in little light and the room would easily have become dark and smoky. A staircase led off the room to the bedroom above, where there was also a fireplace. The lean-to kitchen and bathroom are 20th-century additions. Greycroft was thatched until relatively recently.

John Bond

John Bond (*c.*1819-69) was an agricultural labourer from Stroud who had married Eliza Watts in 1850. Neither were literate. They do not appear to have had any children so would have found the accommodation in Greycroft quite adequate for their needs (unlike the family of eight recorded on the 1841 census). At the side of their inglenook fireplace was a bake oven, used for the baking of bread.

Joseph Draper

Joseph Draper, a carpenter who busied himself mending fences and perhaps other general maintenance, was born *c.*1791 in Stroud. His wife Hannah died in 1839 leaving him to bring up their several children. He moved to Greycroft between 1851 and 1861. At the time of the 1861 census Alfred, his youngest son and two of Joseph's grandchildren were also living or staying in Greycroft, making for cramped sleeping arrangements in the tiny cottage. Joseph died in 1869.

Both Joseph Draper and John Bond were good gardeners and won several prizes during the 1860s at the local shows with their fruit and vegetables. It was essential for them to take full advantage of their extensive garden and orchard. Any surplus produce would have been sold to other villagers.

Walford House

Built in the middle to late 18th century, Walford House was so named by Frederick Walford Vick who bought the property together with Greycroft for £520 in 1882 and lived there until his death in 1909.

Hampden (or Hampton) Bernard Wotton

Hampden (or Hampton) Bernard Wotton came to Walford House in the mid-1860s, staying in Frampton until the early 1870s. Born in Plymouth *c.*1829, he was assistant to the surgeon Thomas Watts. In 1868 the vicar had cause to remember the work of the local medical men at the annual meeting of the Red Scarf Club, for when he had broken his arm earlier that year following a fall from his horse, Hampden Wotton had 'skilfully treated' his injury. The family employed a 13-year-old female servant in 1871 to help look after the house, for Alice Wotton was heavily pregnant with their fourth child.

Wotton was vice-president of the Mechanics' Institute in 1870, and participated in concerts by giving readings, notably the famous speech of Serjeant Buzfuz from *The Pickwick Papers.* Hampden Wotton also entertained the village folk with his singing: 'The comic song "Who's that" by Mr. H.B. Wotton was a decided success, and was rapturously redemanded. The singer substituted another song which was equally pleasing to the audience, and he was compelled to make his third appearance on the platform.'

William Hart (see sketch 49).

48   WOODBINE COTTAGE – undated (probably October 1865)

The cottage is not visible from The Street and is accessed via a private lane.

Henry Hawker and John Millard

Henry Hawker (*c.*1788-1872) was a gardener from Fretherne. He owned a house and garden in The Street from at least 1839 onwards and it may well have been this one. Henry lived with his daughter Ann and her husband John Millard who had 11 children. She inherited the house upon Henry Hawker's death.

John Millard (*c.*1813-1902) was a pit-sawyer. The carpenters and wheelwrights in Frampton would have been dependent on his work once their selected trees had been felled. The heavy trunks were carefully levered into position over the sawpit where they were supported on small

cross-timbers. The top-sawyer stood on the tree trunk to hold his end of the pit-saw, whilst the bottom-sawyer had the unenviable task of standing in the pit below. He would usually wear

a wide-brimmed hat to help keep some of the sawdust from his eyes.

The carpenter or wheelwright would advise his requirements and the sawyer then used twine rubbed with charcoal or chalk to spring against the tree trunk and leave a straight mark along it to show where the cuts should be made. The sawyers took great trouble over sharpening and setting their saws.

John Millard worked with John Evans (of Tudor Cottage) at various farms in Frampton, although by 1871 the heading on the bills was John Millard and Son, rather than John Millard and John Evans. They were employed to do both sawing and general carpentry.

The extract from the *Gloucester Chronicle* helps to illustrate the dangers of travelling on the canal, which frequently claimed the lives of boatmen, passengers, swimmers and people walking on its banks.

NARROW ESCAPE FROM DROWNING.—On Monday evening when the *Lapwing* steamer, which leaves Gloucester for Sharpness Point at five o'clock, was nearing the landing stage at the Six-mile bridge, a sawyer of Frampton named Millard was sitting on the moveable iron rail which bars the side entrance to the deck. With him was his boy, six years old. He was asked to rise, so that the bar might be lifted. He said he would do it himself and did it. Then he seems to have forgotten what he had done, and while about to resume his seat the boat gave a gentle lurch and he toppled over on his back into the canal, and the little boy was taken with him. Father and son sank together, but the father rose and swam towards the bank, forgetting or unaware that his boy had fallen with him. The boy rose, and kept himself at the surface by paddling with his hands. The people on board shouted, and the father turned back as the boy was sinking, and swam with him to the bank. Meantime, two gentlemen on board the steamer — Mr. Rosendal, shipbroker, of this city, and Captain Murphy, of the *Ada*, of Yarmouth, a ship now discharging at this port, had jumped into the water with their clothes on. But the steamer having, of course, advanced, they had to swim some distance, and the father and child were safe on the shore before they could be assisted.

Gloucester Chronicle, 12 August 1865

49   THE STREET (WEST) – 6 October (1865)

Salt Water Row (now Harts Cottages)

These cottages may have been built c.1821 by Henry Brinkworth from Arlingham.

William Hart

William Hart (1812-82) lived, according to the Chapel's Minute Book, 'for many years in the world without God and without hope, but one night overheard his wife praying for his conversion and this incident made so deep an impression on him that he forsook his evil ways and disconnected himself with his business, that of licensed victualler'. He then became a mariner and owned at least two trows which traded on the canal and Severn estuary. William's first wife, Caroline, died in 1873 and he married Anne Jane Manning whereupon he moved to Gloucester and became a methodist. In Frampton William Hart owned the property now known as Cardiff House (see sketch 47) as well as these cottages at Salt Water Row, to which he probably gave his name.

Thomas Dunn

Prior to 1839 Frampton, like all other villages, was policed by parish constables who were elected annually by the Parish Vestry. Their appointment was confirmed by the local magistrates. The number of men appointed varied, and it was by no means a popular office to hold. A constable was unpaid and received expenses only if the perpetrator of the crime were convicted. It was difficult to enforce law and order amongst neighbours and friends and generally it was felt throughout the country that a more organised police force should come into being. The Metropolitan Police Force in London was proving to be a success, and one of its commissioners,

Edwin Chadwick, urged the government to reform its approach towards policing the country by setting up a centrally-organised police force. The resultant Rural Constabulary Act of 1839 was gradually implemented, although some of the counties did not adopt the Act until the middle of the 1850s.

Rural communities were generally sceptical about the Act for two main reasons. The first was that the newly appointed policemen were usually from other parts of the country to avoid being known to the locals, and were thought to be less open to corruption as a result. This led to the non-acceptance of many policemen who had different accents and did not understand the local ways and traditions. (In Frampton there were three policemen on the 1841 census, all living in two houses in Fromebridge.) The second problem related to the need to fund the new force for no one liked to see the inevitable increase in rates that followed.

Numerous petitions greeted the adoption of the 1839 Act in Gloucestershire, Frampton having sent one to the magistrates in January 1842 containing 41 signatures. The majority of the signatories were local farmers (both male and female) and tradesmen of long standing. Among these was the name of Thomas Dunn, a boot and shoemaker.

Thomas Dunn (c.1816-1906) had been born in Haresfield. He married two ladies named Elizabeth, his first wife dying aged 28 in 1842. With a young son to bring up, their baby having died three months after its mother, Thomas soon found another wife, Elizabeth the daughter of Nehemiah Stiff (a local farmer/butcher). They had about fourteen children. The Dunns had moved to Harts Cottages in the mid-1850s.

The family of Thomas Dunn had two further involvements with the police, both in 1862. In September David, one of his sons, witnessed a serious argument between two old women in the village (see sketch 15).

The Dunn family's other brush with the law involved another son, Charles, who in December 1862 was accused of stealing some money from the house of Amelia Allen of Buckholdt Cottages whilst she was at chapel one Sunday evening. All the evidence pointed to Charles Dunn as the thief and he was wearing shoes which made 'very peculiar' footprints and were identical to the footprints found in Amelia Allen's house. (It does not say whether the shoes had been made by his father.) The police decided however that the evidence was not sufficient to convict him (see sketch 19.) Perhaps Thomas Dunn was better disposed towards the paid police force after this incident than he had been twenty years previously?

James Wathen

James Wathen (c.1830-71) was an agricultural labourer from Frampton who married Ellen Hill, her birthplace being variously described as Frampton or Eastington. The couple had no children but in 1861 Ellen's brother Henry Hill was living with them in this cottage. Following the early deaths of James, and Henry's wife Maria, Ellen moved in with her brother to look after his five young children and act as housekeeper.

John Stapleton

John Stapleton (c.1818-79) lived at 1 Salt Marsh Cottages (Splatt) before moving to Harts Cottages, where he was in 1861. A brickmaker from Slimbridge, he married Eliza from Littledean and came to Frampton sometime before 1851. They had four children of which two sons drowned in separate incidents. A third son was a mariner and his wife and children lived with the widowed Eliza for a while. The Stapletons had one daughter, Ann, who transferred from the Chapel School to the National School in 1864. There was always a great rivalry between the two schools to attract pupils, especially when their holidays did not coincide, and children frequently passed from one establishment to the other and back again. The master of the National School regarded the Chapel School as inferior and considered that all its pupils, Ann Stapleton included, were addicted to copying and behind academically.

Ballinger's (now The Old Bakery)

John Ballinger

From approximately the middle of the 1830s John Ballinger (c.1804-76) lived in and ran his bakery business from this house. A native of Frampton, he employed a servant to assist his wife Susan with the general running of the house. However, on one occasion, just two days before this sketch was drawn, his wife found that their latest servant had been dishonest. Susan Ballinger was checking the cash drawer in their bedroom, where about thirty or forty pounds was stored, when she noticed that between three or four pounds was missing. Ann Barnett, a young woman from Rodley, who had been dismissed from their service a few days earlier was arrested and taken to Whitminster Police Station. As was customary, Susan Ballinger was permitted to cross-examine the accused, who confessed to stealing some money and spending it on drapery goods at the nearby shop of Mr. Dodd. She was sentenced to three months hard labour.

For many years George Priday lived with the Ballingers, working as a baker, and it was George who eventually took over the running of the business after John Ballinger died.

William Clarke, John Tilley Ford and Edward Evans (see sketch 15).

50   BLENHEIM HOUSE, THE STREET (WEST) – 6 October (1865)

Margaret Saunders

Margaret Saunders, a schoolmistress, was born in Gloucester *c*.1818 and died in Frampton in 1895. She was widowed early in life and in 1851 was running a school with six boarders at Walford House, just a few doors further down The Street. The number had increased to 12 by 1861.

The school moved to Blenheim House, possibly in 1865, by which time her daughter, Margaret Jane, was helping to teach. They stayed at Blenheim House until sometime between 1881 and 1891, when the ladies moved to the property immediately south of *The Three Horseshoes*. Private schools in Frampton always faced strong competition from the National and Chapel Schools and it is to Margaret Saunders' great credit that her establishment was successful over such a long period of time. Many of her boarders during the 1860s were drawn from nearby villages and all were girls. Boys were taken as day pupils.

Margaret Jane Saunders was in demand both as a pianist and singer at village concerts, being particularly popular at events run by the Mechanics' Institute. She also treasured her copies of the parish magazine, having them bound in annual editions. These have now been deposited in the Gloucestershire Record Office and provide a useful insight into life in Frampton from 1861 onwards.

October 9th Mr Ward. J. Hewlett. Edwin Bowles. Dodd. Peter Coole

51   THE GREEN (WEST) – 9 October 1865

S. Ward, Grocer (now Restaurant on the Green)

Caroline Ward

The Wards were grocers and drapers and for many years ran a shop from these premises, which was also their home. Samuel Ward was born in Market Lavington, the son of Richard Ward, a Congregational minister. He came to live in Frampton *c.*1840 and married Caroline, the eldest daughter of Samuel Rowles, a local ship owner. They had six children before his death in 1861 aged 45.

Caroline Ward took over the running of the shop, her eldest child being 12 years of age. As was the custom, the apprentice was living with the family and would have given her some help. She also had a servant to look after the domestic chores. Mindful of the need to help those less fortunate, she permitted an alms box to be kept on the counter of her shop to relieve the distress in Lancashire, following the crisis in the cotton industry in 1862. The collection amounted to 9 shillings.

The Wards' shop was stocked with a wide range of groceries, from peppercorns to rice, arrowroot to vinegar, currant cakes to mustard, sugar, coffee and tea etc. Household goods such as nightlights, tintacks and oil were also available. It was normal for the more wealthy of the village to run an account which they settled every six months. The drapery side of the business provided villagers with the choice of materials or ready-made clothes, and the furnishing of funerals was a speciality. This meant that mourning attire was also probably available for hire. After a brief illness, Caroline died in 1872 at the age of 48. As was customary, many children

took the day off school to watch the funeral procession as it wound its way through the village to the church.

Caroline Ward had not lived long enough to see her eldest daughter, also Caroline, marry. Her wedding to Frederick Walford Vick, a plumber and decorator, in 1875 was evidently a much-celebrated affair. As the parish magazine reports: 'They were married on a bright sunny day. If the waving of flags and the sound of church bells and explosions of gunpowder can contribute to bliss, this pair should be happy indeed. The bride is so well known and thoroughly respected, and, as we may say, so entirely one of ourselves, that the local enthusiasm needs no explanation to Frampton readers, who will doubtless join their good wishes to our own.'

Brook House
The captioning on the sketch indicates that the artist is referring to Brook House which lies out of sight at the end of the lane through the archway.

James Hewlett

Edward James (known as James) was the son of Edward Hewlett who lived a little further along The Green. Born *c*.1840, a painter and plumber by trade, James Hewlett and his wife Mary Ann had four children before leaving Frampton, probably *c*.1871. Like some of his brothers, he was a singer and performed at several of the local concerts. Brook House was rented by the Hewlett family on a number of occasions. In 1841 it was in the occupation of Daniel Hewlett (an uncle of James and brother of Edward, who also worked as a sculptor) when he was running a school from the property, and there is evidence of the old schoolroom on the first floor. Known then as Beehive Academy, it presumably took its name from the stone beehive over the door. Twelve 'young gentlemen' with ages ranging from 7 to 14 are included on the census. It may have been the forerunner of the Chapel School which opened in 1849 as over the years the house seems to have had many connections with the Congregational Church, and was the home of its minister, the Rev. Thomas Clegg, in 1871.

The last members of the Hewlett family to live in Brook House were Emma Margaret and Thomas who died in 1921 and 1928 respectively. Thomas was a brother of James Hewlett, featured in this sketch.

Clarence House

Edwin Rowles

Edwin Rowles (c.1803-82) was born in Arlingham, the brother of Samuel Rowles who lived in Buckholdt. Edwin, his wife Eliza and their three surviving children settled in Frampton in the early 1840s, living in the house shown. He owned several properties in the village including, towards the latter part of his life, Brook House (described above). Edwin and Eliza's annual contribution of £1 0s. 0d. towards the running of the National School may not seem much today, but they were among the more benevolent donors of their time.

> **FRAMPTON-ON-SEVERN.**
> **T**O be LET, with immediate possession,—Two well fitted up HOUSES, containing 6 Rooms each, with Gardens, and both sorts of Water. Rent moderate. For further particulars apply to Mr. Edwin Rawles, Frampton-on-Severn, Gloucestershire.

Gloucester Journal, 18 July 1868

Like Samuel Rowles, Edwin was a successful barge owner. His son, Richard Carter Doctor Rowles became a master mariner and was bequeathed all Edwin's sailing vessels, and house, warehouse and wharf at Newnham. His real estate and personal property was divided between Richard and his daughter Mary Ann Rowles.

John Dodd

The Dodd family were only in Frampton during the first half of the 1860s. They are traceable via the annual trade directories which list the main inhabitants of the village and tradesmen. In the 1863 *Post Office Directory*, John Dodd is included as a grocer. Thomas Henry Dodd, a grocer of Frampton, appeared in the *Morris and Co. Directory* of 1865-6. The advertisements for Cassell's Coffee in the *Gloucester Journals* of 1862-6 list J.H. Dodd of Frampton on Severn among their agents. Thomas Henry Dodd was also a Collector of Land Tax in 1863 but at a meeting of the Vestry in January 1865 it was noted that he had left the parish without fulfilling all his duties.

The Three Horseshoes

Peter Coole

Peter Coole was one of the village's blacksmiths. Born c.1798 in South Cerney, he and his wife Mary lived in Frampton from the early 1830s and can be traced in the Register of Electors from 1839 onwards as owning the property depicted and its garden.

He was certainly retailing beer by 1854 (and possibly earlier), although his main trade remained that of blacksmith. In the 1860s *The Three Horseshoes* was one of the most appropriately named properties in Frampton. Peter Coole was also a keen gardener and rented an allotment for a guinea per annum from Henry Clifford Clifford for many years.

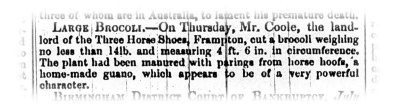

three of whom are in Australia, to lament his premature death.

LARGE BROCOLI.—On Thursday, Mr. Coole, the landlord of the Three Horse Shoes, Frampton, cut a brocoli weighing no less than 14lb. and measuring 4 ft. 6 in. in circumference. The plant had been manured with parings from horse hoofs, a home-made guano, which appears to be of a very powerful character.

Gloucester Journal, 29 July 1854

In that same year Peter Coole tendered for the contract to make a boundary fence around the churchyard. His quotation of £304 0s. 0d. (some £63 cheaper than his nearest rival) was accepted and he later carried out the work. In 1866 he took part in a 'foot-race' contesting a distance of a mile with his near neighbour George Hobbs. He was, by then, over sixty and weighed some seventeen stone (see page 119 for the result).

Mary Coole died in 1870 and Peter then employed a housekeeper before retiring and remarrying in 1872. He moved to Purton, Wilts, leaving his son William to run both his businesses. Peter Coole died of liver failure in 1879.

James Watkins

On the 1881 census the property formed part of Collingwood Terrace but the origin of this name is not clear.

James Watkins (*c*.1819-1905) was an agricultural labourer at the time of the sketch, but he later became a barber in Frampton. Although James was born in Ross-on-Wye, his parents had married in Frampton and were only away from the village for a few years before returning in the early 1820s. His father was Frampton's tallow chandler. James married twice, his wives bearing him a total of 13 children. This must have put a heavy strain on the family's finances and Eliza, his second wife, appears to have found it necessary to work first as a laundress and then a charwoman. The Watkins lived in the cottage next to *The Three Horseshoes* from sometime before the 1851 census until at least 1891.

George Hewlett

George Hewlett (*c*.1798-1876) was born in Frampton and he married again after Mary, his first, wife died. He was an agricultural labourer who was later a fruiter (fruit grower) and then a carrier. Ann (his second wife) was a shopkeeper. They had one son, also called George, who became a labourer. Although living just two doors away from Edward Hewlett, the two families were not particularly closely related.

Mary Ricketts

Mary Ricketts (*c*.1786-1878) was the widow of John Ricketts, who had died on 26 March 1865, a few months before the sketch was drawn. John Ricketts, born *c*.1773, served as a marine in the Battle of the Nile (1798) and the Capture of Copenhagen (1801). In the interlude of peace he may have been paid off as he appears to have joined the local Sea Fencibles in 1803 in order to assist with the defence of the country from attack by sea at a time when Napoleon posed a threat of invasion. He later returned to the navy, fought at Trafalgar (1805), and was wounded in an engagement with a Russian Frigate off Cronstadt, in the Baltic Sea. Following retirement from active service, John Ricketts was a butcher.

FRAMPTON-ON-SEVERN. — *Marriage Festivities.* — On Tuesday, the 23d instant, this village was the scene of a gay wedding. The parties were Mr. Job Dodwell, of Bridgend, Glamorgan, South Wales, and Phœbe, only child of the gallant naval veteran, Mr. John Ricketts. The church was prettily decorated with festoons and garlands of flowers. The path of the bridal party was strewed with flowers by the girls of the National School. On the return of the party to the residence of the bride's father, a large circle of friends sat down to a sumptuous *dejeuner*. The health of the happy pair was proposed by the Rev. M. F. St. John. The girls of the school were regaled with cake, which the fair bride, with her accustomed affability, herself dispensed.

Gloucester Journal, 27 October 1860

The Ricketts' daughter Phoebe was married in 1860 and an account of her wedding appeared in the *Gloucester Journal*.

Prior to his death at the age of 91, John Ricketts had been the oldest inhabitant of Frampton and a very active member of the church. It was said that almost until the end he walked with the ease of a man of sixty.

Runton Cottage

Edward Hewlett

Edward Hewlett, born *c.*1803, was a son of Daniel Hewlett who built the Congregational Church in Frampton. They are both commemorated on the upstairs wall of the chapel, together with Edward's brother, also called Daniel, who worked as a sculptor on the restoration of Lichfield Cathedral under Sir Gilbert Scott.

The Hewlett family had moved to Frampton from Wheatenhurst (now part of Whitminster) during the late 1700s and were, in the main, carpenters. The generation before Edward had held positions of responsibility within the parishes and had accumulated some land and property. Daniel, Edward's father, had owned the area now known as Wards Court, but this was all gradually sold off after his death to pay for the bringing up, educating and apprenticing of his many children.

Edward married Mary Ann Workman, also from Frampton, in 1832 and they had eight children, the first two dying in infancy. He and his family lived in several properties in Frampton and he was probably the first occupier of the former workhouse (now Stockelm Cottage) in 1837 after it had closed. He came to Runton Cottage sometime before 1861 and lived there probably until his death in 1876, after being paralysed for three years.

Edward followed the family trade of carpenter and evidence of payment for his work is found in the Overseer's accounts books of the parish; this includes the making of coffins. He also tendered for replacing the pews in the parish church in 1854 along with John Burr, a local cabinet maker. Their quotation of £470 0s. 0d. was the second lowest, but it is not known whether it was accepted.

A loyal supporter of the Royal Family, he, along with his neighbour George Hobbs, decorated their houses and the adjoining Mechanics' Institute with 'a series of floral emblems and devices' during the celebrations for the wedding of the Prince of Wales in 1863. Today Edward's great grandson, Thomas Joseph Hewlett (the author's father), has in his possession a newspaper commemorating the Coronation of Queen Victoria in 1837. It is thought that this originally belonged to Edward.

During the 1860s Charles Hewlett, one of Edward's sons, was a pupil teacher at the National School. After passing his Government examinations he became master of Oakridge National School near Stroud. He maintained his links with Frampton's school by assisting with the teaching during his holidays (often those of Oakridge and Frampton were different) and became master at Frampton from 1878 to 1881.

Severnthorpe

George Hobbs

George Hobbs (*c*.1817-85), a butcher by trade, was born in Woodchester and married Eliza who came from Down Hatherley. They appear to have arrived in Frampton during the mid-1840s.

George and Eliza suffered the loss of three of their children within the space of seven weeks in the summer of 1854 owing to an outbreak of scarlet fever that killed 18 youngsters in the village over a 10-week period. George's children were aged eight months, three and six years; the eldest dying from a secondary fever caught after she had contracted scarlet fever. The disease is characterised by a fever, strawberry-coloured tongue and a red rash that starts on the neck and chest and spreads to the abdomen and limbs. Those lucky enough to survive scarlet fever would then have found their skin peeling off for several weeks. In the 19th century it was highly feared. Nowadays it is a relatively uncommon disease and is usually cured by treatment with penicillin. George and Eliza's eldest daughter survived the outbreak, and the couple later had two more children.

George, like Edward Hewlett next door, was a keen gardener and won prizes for his green plums and vegetables at the first of the Frampton and Fretherne Cottage Gardeners' Society shows in 1863. He was also a singer, regularly entertaining members of the Mechanics' Institute whose premises were next door to his own.

Eliza Hobbs died in 1874, a few years before her husband. Her funeral was held on the same day as the Harvest Festival that year. The bells were silent apart from their usual chiming as the large congregation walked home after the harvest thanksgiving, meeting the funeral procession on its way to the church. The loss of 'a valued parishioner' was greeted with sorrow and all the gladness of the harvest 'was sobered with feelings of sympathy for the bereaved family'.

FRAMPTON-ON-SEVERN. — An exciting foot-race came off at this place, on Monday last, between Mr. Peter Coole, of the Horse-shoe Inn, and Mr. G. Hobbs, butcher. The race was one mile for 50 sovereigns, and resulted in Mr. Hobbs being the winner. Mr. Coole is upwards of 60 years of age, and weighs something like 17 stone, and the other gentleman was suffering from a recent attack of the gout.

Gloucester Journal, 31 March 1866

Literary and Mechanics' Institute (now the Hairdressers)

In November 1852, Thomas Watts (senior) of The Grange founded the Literary and Mechanics' Institute in Frampton. A believer in self-education, he felt that the working classes should spend their leisure time reading and studying in a manner that was pleasing to God. Held in high regard in the community, Thomas Watts led the Institute members for just a couple of years before he died in 1855. His popularity is evident from the many newspaper reports which give details of the activities. By the end of the first year the Institute had 75 members, and patrons and friends, including a large number of ladies, were frequently in attendance at meetings and concerts. The Rules were designed to ensure that everyone was

FRAMPTON-ON-SEVERN.

RULES OF THE

LITERARY AND MECHANICS' INSTITUTE.

1st.—That the object of this Institution shall be to provide facilities for self-improvement, and the diffusion of scientific and general knowledge, by means of a Reading Room, Library, and occasional Lectures.

2nd.—That the business of the Society shall commence on the first day of November, 1852, and that no Member's Subscription shall be less than sixpence per month.

3rd.—That each Member shall pay, upon entrance, one month in advance, and the like sum on the first day of every succeeding month, by taking it to the Secretary; and no Member shall be allowed to enter the Room until his Subscription is paid up.

4th.—That the business of the Institution shall be conducted by a Committee of Twelve Members—viz., a President, Vice-President, Treasurer, Secretary, and eight others, who are to be annually elected on the first day of November in every year; but any Member of the Committee may be re-elected; and six of such Committee shall constitute a quorum.

5th.—That the Library shall consist of Newspapers, Magazines, and Books, to be purchased by the Committee, or presented or lent by the Members or other persons.

6th.—That the Reading Room shall be open every day in the week, from 10 o'clock in the morning until 10 at night, except Sundays and Christmas Day; and that all arrangements relative to the purchase of Furniture, Newspapers, Magazines, Books, and other matters of business, shall be made and transacted by the Committee from time to time, as occasion may require.

7th.—That the Committee shall meet on the first Tuesday in every month, at some convenient place to be appointed by them, at 7 o'clock in the evening, for the purpose of general business.

8th.—That the Committee shall have the power of expelling any Member for misconduct, but such Member shall have his last month's subscription returned to him.

9th.—That any person wishing to become a Member shall apply to the Secretary, who shall state the name of such person to the Committee at their next meeting, and they shall either admit or refuse him, as the majority may think proper.

10th.—That no Newspaper, Book, or any Publication shall be taken out of the Reading Room without the permission of the Secretary, who shall have the care thereof.

11th.—That no Member shall retain a Newspaper more than half an hour after another Member has expressed a wish to have it.

12th.—That if any Member shall enter the Room in a state of intoxication, and shall refuse to leave it on being requested by one of the Committee, he shall be compelled so to do, and fined one shilling; and if the fine be not paid in a week, he shall be expelled.

13th.—That, as it is very essential that good order and decorous and courteous behaviour shall be strictly observed amongst the Members at their respective meetings, should any one of them introduce political or sectarian discussion, or use offensive, provoking, or improper language to another Member, and persist therein after being called to order by the President, he shall be fined half-a-crown.

14th.—That on no account shall any fermented liquors or smoking be introduced into the Room; and any Member so offending shall be fined half-a-crown.

15th.—The President shall be entitled to a casting vote, in addition to his vote as a Member.

16th.—That the Treasurer's Accounts shall be audited once in every year.

17th.—That the Secretary shall give notice of all General and Special Meetings; he shall record Minutes of the Proceedings at all Committee and General Meetings; receive and enter the Subscriptions and Names of the Members in proper Books to be provided for that purpose; pay over to the Treasurer at every Monthly Meeting of the Committee all Monies in his hands belonging to the Institution; and conduct the general business thereof, so far as the same is consistent with these Rules and the Resolutions of the Committee.

18th.—All Monies in the hands of the Treasurer shall be at the disposal of the Committee, for the benefit of the Institution.

19th.—The Committee shall be at liberty to make such Bye Laws and minor Regulations for the government of the Institution as are not inconsistent with its Constitution and Rules.

20th.—That any Member shall be at liberty to introduce a Friend into the Room occasionally, provided such friend be not a constant resident in Frampton.

21st.—That this Institution shall not be broken up or dissolved unless by the consent of at least three-fourths of the Members who shall be present at a Special General Meeting to be called for that purpose; and no Member shall be entitled to vote at such Meeting unless he shall have been a Member for one year, and paid up his Subscriptions.

President..................THOMAS WATTS, Esq.
Vice-President............Mr. WILLIAM HORNER.
Treasurer..................Mr. THOMAS BELLAMY BARNARD.
Secretary..................Mr. JOHN BURR.

W. Henley, Printer, Cross, Gloucester.

given the opportunity to read the many books and newspapers that were either bought or donated.

In the 1860s a large membership continued to enjoy the annual tea meetings and lectures and during the winter months a series of soirées were held where individuals or groups entertained with music and readings. A variety of topics were discussed at the lectures including China and the Chinese, Geology, The French Revolution of 1789, True Manliness and Rome. The Literary and Mechanics' Institute certainly provided the opportunity of learning to a rural population who wanted to know more about the world they lived in, its history and the topical issues of the day.

Richard Stiff (see sketch 52).

52   THE GREEN (WEST) – 9 October 1865

Sunny Side

Richard Stiff

Richard Stiff (*c*.1822-78) was married to Ann, the daughter of a local shoemaker, Daniel King. Originally a baker, Richard suddenly found himself having to run Advowson Farm following the death of his father, Nehemiah Stiff, in 1864. It was an occupation in which he was to continue throughout the rest of his life, his bakery business passing to William James Whittard, the husband of his niece.

The Stiffs do not appear to have had any children, so Richard's will concentrated on bequests to many members of his and Ann's families, all resident in Frampton. He was the owner of several properties in the village, notably three cottages at The Lake, *The True Heart* (which at the time was a beerhouse of that name), and three cottages on The Green situated at the entrance of the lane to the chapel (now the site of Roe's Pool House) which his wife Ann had inherited following the death of her father. The executors of Richard's will and trustees of his estate were his friends George Cooper Bubb, the farmer at Nastfield, and Charles Neale, a pork butcher. The task of trustee was often an onerous one lasting many years, particularly if they oversaw the management of properties left in trust. If it was still ongoing when the trustee himself died the duties passed to the trustee's trustees.

Kempsey House

William Knight

William Knight (born in Saul *c*.1822) was a master mariner and moved to this house from Fretherne sometime during the late 1850s. Married to Ann, who came from Woodchester, he had at least six children. Living with the family during the 1860s was Mary Small (also from Woodchester) who was probably Ann's mother.

Melbourne Knight, the youngest child, got into trouble with his parents and the schoolmaster when, rather than purchasing a copybook, he spent the money given to him elsewhere, presumably on his way to school. The Catechism was taught every Friday at the National School, the children having either to recite it each week or answer questions about it. Many parents were not happy with this arrangement and attendance on a Friday was almost always depleted as a result. William and Ann Knight addressed the issue by writing to the master

asking that Melbourne not learn the Catechism as they did not attend church; a request that he seems to have respected. (This is a rare example of what might be interpreted as tension between the Anglican and nonconformist elements in the village.)

Site of Roe's Pool House
The property appears to be one of the three cottages that were on the site of Roe's Pool House.

Wilkins

Although there were several families of Wilkins in the village during the 1860s it is not clear who was living in this property in 1865. It was possibly Elizabeth Wilkins (born *c.*1801 in Kidderminster, Worcs.), the widow of William, a tailor.

Chapel House
Situated at the end of the lane leading to the chapel, Chapel House is not visible in the sketch.

Noah Spire

Noah Spire lived in the property from sometime before 1861, having previously come from Standish and Haresfield. Born in Hardwicke *c.*1807, he was a butcher by trade. His second wife Emma came from Frampton. The couple had at least five children and these seem to have been educated at both main schools in the village. One of them even tried out the British School at Saul for a short while, the family having objected to the beating he received at the National School. Noah Spire died in 1874 and Emma a year later.

The Green. From The Bell Inn, priory. Higgins Ivy Cottage. Oct 9th

Congregational Church

In 1662 the fourth Act of Uniformity was passed requiring that church services were conducted according to the revised prayer book and liturgy of the Church of England. Around 2,000 clergy were ejected from their livings for not conforming to the Act, among them John Barnsdale, the vicar of Frampton. The Rev. Barnsdale was the first nonconformist of the parish of whom there is any known record. He held secret services on the banks of the Severn and was lucky that no one reported him to the authorities for, had he been caught, the penalty would have probably been execution. In 1689 the Toleration Act granted nonconformists the right to have their own places of worship, together with teachers and preachers. With no chapel, the nonconformists of Frampton met in houses, farms and in public places such as Fitcherbury. Among the speakers was the Rev. Rowland Hill, a well-known preacher in the area, and through his influence arrangements were made for the erection of a chapel. This was built in 1776 by Daniel Hewlett, a young man of 21 years. He and his family lived in nearby Wheatenhurst (Whitminster), his grandfather and great grandfather both having held the position of parish clerk there. At an early age Daniel found an interest in the nonconformist movement and his second and third wives (sisters) came from a large nonconformist family in Dursley by the name of Rudder. The chapel was his only major building work. The Hewlett family were carpenters and it is likely that Daniel's son Edward was involved in the alterations of 1857 when the chapel was repewed, and a new reading desk and gallery were added. The schoolroom was added in 1849.

The minister of the chapel during the early 1860s was the Rev. William Lewis (1816–98). Ordained in 1843, William Lewis had actually started his ministry in the village a couple of years earlier working alongside the Rev. William Richardson before the latter's retirement. He and his young family lived in Lake House. During his time in the village he had done much for the chapel and its members, but life had not always been easy. He had to live with the almost supreme power of the Established Church which had a large revenue to distribute, much influence over village matters, and a considerable number of people willing to support it financially. Attendance at the chapel had, on the whole, been well kept up, but there was always the problem of young adults leaving the village to seek labour elsewhere and the death of elderly members. The Rev. Lewis had a conciliatory nature and did his best to work beside the Rev. St John at the parish church. One of their greatest acts of unity was their fight for temperance. Tea Meetings were a regular feature of chapel life and they were followed either by talks of a religious nature, or readings and musical performances. These events and the regular services attracted a large number of people, not only from Frampton, but also the surrounding villages.

The Rev. Lewis was acknowledged as a good preacher; sometimes using notes and sometimes not, he was forthright and persuasive in his teaching. When the Independent Chapel at Lytham in Lancashire was opened in 1862 he was among those ministers asked to officiate. The trustees at Lytham were so impressed with him that two years later they asked him to become their minister. The decision to leave Frampton was a difficult one, for William Lewis had thought that he would be spending the rest of his days in Gloucestershire, but his doctors advised him that on health grounds he should move to another residence.

Members of the chapel gave the Rev. Lewis a farewell Tea Meeting one Monday afternoon in June 1864. The schoolroom was tastefully decorated with 'cut flowers and appropriate mottoes'. About 150 people took tea after which they, and others, assembled in the chapel for a public meeting. The senior deacon, Edward Morgan, was voted to the chair and spoke on behalf of all present expressing his sadness at the departure of the Rev. Lewis who had served the chapel for 23 years. A presentation purse containing £37 10s. was received by the minister amid much emotion. The Rev. Lewis reflected on the renovations to the chapel and in particular the eradication of the dry rot, which he hoped would never reach the pulpit!

The Rev. Thomas Clegg (born c.1826) succeeded William Lewis as minister during the late 1860s. He appears to have taken the members through a relatively quiet period of the chapel's history before leaving in the early 1870s to take up his ministry in Charfield. In January 1875 the Rev. William Lewis returned to Frampton to resume his duties at the chapel until his retirement in 1879.

Hannah Frape

This relates to another of the cottages that were originally on the site of Roe's Pool House.
The caption 'Mrs Frape' probably refers to Hannah Frape, the widow of Joseph, a groom. Hannah Frape (c.1813-1904), a laundress, came from the Nailsworth area. She and Joseph had at least five children and one of them, Powell, highlighted a problem that the schoolmaster often had with his pupils: 'Jan. 13th 1863 – The boys in the 2nd class especially P. Frape (and others) do very well both in arithmetic and dictation and would doubtless exhibit a very satisfactory result next Inspection could their parents be induced to send them'.

Cant Leaze

Samuel Lawrence

Samuel Lawrence was born c.1834 in Saul. He was a master mariner and appears to have only lived in Frampton from the mid-1860s to early 1870s with his wife Elizabeth and their young children.

53 Entrance to Frampton Court from Perry Way

Entrance Gate to Frampton Court.   *August 23/66*

Poole House

Ann Smith

Ann Smith, born *c.*1789 in Moreton Valence, was the widow of Samuel Smith, a builder. After his death she carried on Samuel's business for a short while, but was later described as a proprietor of houses. She died in Stroud in 1879, and was buried in Frampton, leaving several properties in the village to her daughters.

Mallard Cottage

John Powell

John Powell was born in Herefordshire *c.*1798. A tailor, he married Esther (or Hester) who came from Berkeley and they had at least five children. Living first at Salt Water Row (now Harts Cottages) in 1841, they moved to this cottage before 1851. John died in 1873.

Ridgwood

Hobbs (see sketch 16; these two families may have been identified the wrong way around)

It is possible that this cottage was occupied by Hannah, the widow of William Hobbs, a waterman born sometime around the beginning of the 19th century.

Thomas Bennett (see sketch 3); George Bennett and William Wood (see sketch 4); Thomas Karn (see sketch 5); Joseph Priday and William Higgins (see sketch 6).

53   ENTRANCE TO FRAMPTON COURT FROM PERRY WAY
– 23 August 1866

The entrance gates to The Park at Frampton Court with Perry Way Lodge (now Park Lodge) on the left. During the 1860s Park Lodge was occupied, at various times, by William Jones (born *c*.1802 in Shropshire), gardener to Henry Clifford Clifford, and Moses Smith (*c*.1813-91), an agricultural labourer and carter. The property may well have been empty when this sketch was drawn.

54   PERRY WAY – 23 August 1866

Perrymead Cottage

Hannah Draper and Thomas Turner

Hannah Draper (*c*.1813-88) was born in Eastington. Following the death of her husband she struggled to bring up her two young children being described as 'pauper' on the 1851 census. By the early 1860s her situation had improved; she was a sempstress (seamstress) and her children Daniel and Elizabeth were a butcher and house servant respectively. Hannah later married Thomas Turner (*c*.1813-84), an agricultural labourer from Hasfield who was her lodger throughout the 1860s.

Perryway Cottage

Henry Morgan

Henry (*c*.1821-1908) was a son of John Morgan who had lived at The Laurels in The Street (west). Like other members of his family he became a bricklayer and builder and this trade was

passed on to his two eldest sons. Henry and his wife Maria's youngest boy, Edgar Samuel, was a pupil teacher at the National School, who started his five year apprenticeship in 1869 at a wage of £6 per annum. An able sportsman, Edgar played cricket and football for the village and was often allowed to miss his duties at school when playing in cricket matches either on The Green or in The Park at Frampton Court.

Henry was a member of the Mechanics' Institute and gave readings at their regular soirées. These evenings proved extremely popular among the folk at Frampton and were held mainly during the winter months. They consisted of recitations, readings, songs, glees, choruses and other musical items. From the newspaper reports it appears that the villagers were a talented group who were very appreciative of each other's efforts and achievements.

55   THE TURNPIKE, PERRY WAY – undated

The turnpike was situated almost opposite the lane to Fromebridge, on the Perry Way.

According to the 1861 census the turnpike toll collector was Lewis Walker. Having been born in Wotton-under-Edge *c*.1813, he lived with his wife Maria and their son Joseph, an agricultural labourer, aged 12. Ten years later the census enumerator recorded Charles Jobbins, an 81-year-old from Shropshire as the turnpike gatekeeper.

56   TOWNFIELD FARM – undated

Richard Hewer

Richard Hewer, born in Kempsford *c.*1829, came to Townfield Farm sometime before 1861 as Henry Clifford Clifford's farm bailiff, and his sister Fanny kept house for him. (The bailiff acted on behalf of the landlord and would have kept a close eye on unlawful happenings occurring on the Clifford estate. There was little poaching reported in the newspapers, and no evidence of a gamekeeper living in Frampton either on the 1861 or 1871 census. However, it seems likely that some poaching must have taken place in the village). In addition to the Frampton Fat Cattle and Sheep Fair held annually on the third Tuesday of February, farmers had the opportunity of selling and buying at similar events in Whitminster and also privately arranged auctions. There was a sale at

Gloucester Journal, 14 September 1867

TOWNFIELD FARM, FRAMPTON-ON-SEVERN,
Three miles from Frocester, 4 from Stonehouse, on
the Midland Railway, and 9 from Gloucester.

Highly Important Sale of a FLOCK *of* 345 PURE-BRED
SUSSEX DOWNS, 135 *Highly Superior* CROSS-BRED
LAMBS, 25 *Two and Three-year-old* STEERS, 7
WAGGON HORSES, STEAM-ENGINE, BOILER,
THRASHING MACHINE, *variety of Modern* FARM-
ING IMPLEMENTS, *Iron Rick Staddles*, CAR-
RIAGES, HARNESS, &c.

BRUTON and KNOWLES
Are favoured with instructions from the Executors of the
late H. C. CLIFFORD, Esq.

TO SELL BY AUCTION,
On Tuesday, September 24th, 1867, commencing punctually
at twelve o'clock,—

189 Splendid Pure-bred Young SUSSEX
DOWN EWES,
50 Splendid SUSSEX DOWN THEAVES,
105 LAMBS, and two-shear pure-bred SUSSEX
DOWN RAM,
135 Highly Superior Cross-bred WETHER and
CHILVER LAMBS,
2 COTSWOLD RAMS, bred by Mr. Barton,
25 Fresh Two and Three-year-old SHORTHORN
STEERS,
7 WAGON HORSES, (excellent workers,)
Brougham, 2 Phaetons, Dog Cart, Double and Single Har-
ness, Saddles, 8 Sets of Long and Trace Harness, 7 Horse-
power Steam Engine and Boiler, Thrashing Machine, Chaff
ditto, Oat Crusher, together with the whole of the Shafting,
Bearings, &c. by *Ferrabee*; 8 Narrow-wheel Carts, with
Portable Scotch, Harvest Beds; *Croskill's* Clod Crusher;
Iron Roller; Wheat and Turnip Drills; Horse Hoe, by
Howard; Cultivator; *Howard's* Ploughs and Harrows,
Sheep Dipping Apparatus, by *Biggs*; 18 Iron Rick
Staddles, Weighing Machine, Oil Cake Crusher, 80 Speckled
Hamburgh, Dorking and Spanish Fowls, 13 East India
Ducks, &c.

*The Sheep, which are remarkably healthy, and of first-class
quality, are descended from the eminent Flocks of the late
Jonas Webb, Esq. Earl Bathurst, Earl Ducie, and Colonel
Kingscote.*

Luncheon will be on the table at eleven, and the Sale will
commence with the Sheep most punctually at twelve o'clock.

Catalogues may be obtained at the Bell Inn, Frampton;
Crown and Anchor, Stonehouse; Spread Eagle and Fleece
Hotels, and of the Auctioneers, King Street, Gloucester.

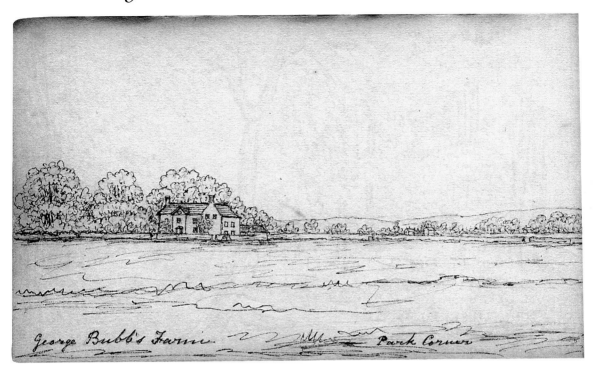

George Bubb's Farm. *Park Corner*

Townfield of 'unusually prime and superior quality' bullocks and 'very ripe' sheep of 'nice weights' two days before the death of Henry Clifford Clifford, the owner of the farm, in 1867.

H.C. Clifford's heir, his grandson Henry James Clifford, decided to sell the farm which until that date had been run as a 'home farm' on the family's estate. The money realised was not as great as anticipated and Richard Hewer, who continued as the tenant farmer until 1877, acquired many bargains at the sale. He employed 9 men and 2 boys to work the 240 acres according to the 1871 census.

57 NASTFIELD FARM – undated

Nastfield farmhouse was built during the mid- to late 18th century, and certainly by 1777.

George Cooper Bubb

George Cooper Bubb was born *c.*1831 probably at Nastfield, and, following the death of his father Henry in 1860, took over the running of the farm. According to the 1851 census Henry Bubb had employed 14 labourers, 10 men, three women and a boy. By 1881 George's workforce was only three labourers and three boys, the reduction being due, in all probability, to the increased use of mechanical implements, several years of poor weather and the end of the 'golden age of farming'.

However, during the 1860s much of the work would still have been done by hand. The farm servants started work as early as 4a.m. during harvest time in order to prepare the horses for their labours during the day. At dusk the servants were required to look after the horses once again, feeding and making them comfortable for the night, before snatching a few hours of well-earned rest.

B. Watts.   *The Parks Farm. Aug.ᵗ 18.ᵗʰ 1866.*   *Frocester Church.*

The labourers arrived at work by 6a.m. during the summer, and 7a.m. (or first light) in the winter. Working through to 6p.m. or dusk, depending on the time of the year, they looked forward to the one-and-a-half hour lunch-break in the middle of the day. The farmers supplied their labourers with a drink of ale or cider, and at harvest time it was not unusual to see a barrel at the corner of the field from which the workers helped themselves. The daily allowance of drink was in the region of half a gallon, or even more, and traditionally formed part of the labourer's wages. In 1879, when the Temperance Movement had become active in the village, the vicar tried to persuade farmers to provide an oatmeal drink for their workforce. When the drink allowance was eventually made illegal by the Truck Act of 1887, there was much opposition across England, workers preferring their daily refreshment to an increase in wages.

The ale and cider helped wash down the midday meal of bread and cheese taken, no doubt, under the shade of some of Frampton's many trees during the good weather. In the winter the labourers would tramp along muddy lanes to the fields, icy winds biting at their faces, with frozen hands and feet covered in chilblains. Sometimes the weather was too bad to work, and those employed on a daily basis faced the prospect of no wages until the rain and snow had gone. It was during these winter months that the families were most vulnerable to poverty, and the ill health that lack of proper nourishment brings.

Farmers like George Bubb were ever mindful of the need to support the less fortunate; they had a vested interest in looking after their labourers during these times for they needed them fit and well during the rest of the year. Together with another farmer, Thomas Browning, George was a Guardian of the Poor for most of the 1860s. The Guardians were in charge of the local administration of poor relief. George Bubb also subscribed to the local charities which were set up to help the poor with the provision of free coal etc. and was a financial

Long-down. Peak-down.

supporter of the National School, believing that the opportunity of education should be given to every child. Following a stroke and several years of bad health George Bubb died in 1892, leaving a personal estate of almost £3,500 to his widow Mary Jane, in trust for their three children.

58   PARKS FARM – 18 August 1866

The building may date to the mid- or late 16th century. Its original identity was largely removed two centuries later when several farm buildings were also added.

Edward Watts

Edward Watts farmed at Parks Farm from Lady Day 1859. (Traditionally tenancies were renewed or exchanged on 25 March, Lady Day.) To help him look after the 238 acres he employed four men, one boy and a dairymaid. His brother George lived with him, assisting on the farm.

WANTED, in a Farm-House, — A YOUNG PERSON, to teach and take the entire charge of four little Boys, the eldest not 10, and to make herself generally useful. A Church person preferred.
Address, E. Watts, The Parks Farm, Frampton-on-Severn, Stonehouse.

Gloucester Journal, 14 February 1863

FIRE AT FRAMPTON.—On Tuesday evening a fire broke out in a wheat rick belonging to Mr. E. Watts, at Park's Farm. Ann Davies, a servant of Mr. Watts, first saw the fire, and raised an alarm, when Mr. G. Watts, and a labourer who was in the house, with others who arrived, commenced carrying water to extinguish it, while some threw rick cloths over the adjacent ricks, about eight in number, and thus prevented their becoming ignited. The fire was not extinguished until about half the rick was destroyed, and the remainder of it rendered almost worthless. Mr. Supt. Griffin, with the police at Whitminster, made enquiries to ascertain the cause of the fire. The rick yard is within a few yards of the house, and before the fire broke out the Carter and Boy had been in the rick yard fetching hay for the horses, and one of them admitted to Mr. Griffin that he sometimes smoked about the premises unknown to his master, but denied taking any light in the yard. Tied up ten yards from the rick was a very savage dog, and nearer the house another, which always makes a noise at strangers. The Superintendent was informed that the dogs did not make the least noise before the fire broke out, which must have been the case had any strangers come into the rick yard; there can therefore be but little doubt but the fire was accidentally caused by some of the workmen carrying a light or smoking in the rick yard. It was fortunate the fire was discovered so soon, and but for the assistance rendered by those present, to whom much credit is due, the other ricks with the buildings would in all probability have been destroyed. Mr. Watts came to this city about half-past nine o'clock, to inform Mr. Jeens, the agent for the Liverpool and London Office, of the disaster. Mr. Watts had recently insured his property in this office. He intimated that the fire engines were not required, but Mr. Jeens thought it prudent to take the Phœnix engine in case of any further mishap, and the Norwich engine, which had been got ready, would have also started, but was stopped by Mr. Watts and Mr. Jeens. The damage done will amount to about 50*l.* or 60*l.*

THE RAILWAY RIOT AT WORCESTER. — On

Gloucester Journal, 13 December 1862

Edward Watts was born *c.*1825. The family came from Slimbridge where his first three children had been born after his marriage to Susanna. He regularly enjoyed coursing on the New Grounds at Slimbridge (near the site of the present Wildfowl and Wetlands Trust) and the day would end with dinner at the *White Lion Inn*, Cambridge. Edward Watts was a keen member of the church and also one of the churchwardens.

Whether or not the children were educated at home is not clear, but just over a year later the three eldest boys were admitted to the National School from 'a private school'. Aged 11, 10 and 8 years they were unable to write down numbers from dictation, and their arrival in the second class caused the master some consternation as he had to revise the first four rules of arithmetic for their benefit. A few weeks later they were absent for two months having contracted smallpox, a highly feared disease. (Although vaccination was available in the 1860s it was not until 1871 and 1872 that mass vaccination programmes were noted in the school records.)

Fromebridge

The small hamlet of Fromebridge (or Froombridge), a couple of miles to the north-east of Frampton, comprised two farms, a mill and several small cottages. The close-knit community were employed mainly within Fromebridge, and few outsiders worked there.

The mill appears to have been used during the 19th century for clothmaking, and there was definitely a cloth factory at Fromebridge in the 1860s, which was probably housed in the tall central block of the mill buildings and lit with ranges of large windows. Some of the workers may have worked from their homes, particularly through the earlier part of the century, as there is evidence of 'loom windows' (large windows through which the looms were taken and which also gave much-needed light to the weavers) on a couple of the cottages.

The mill was used principally for the production of flour for human consumption together with, almost certainly, cereals for animal feedstuffs. Working hours varied according to the time of year and flow of water, of which Fromebridge was generally blessed with a good supply. During idle periods the workers would have been employed in general maintenance and repairs around the mill, or clearing out the millstream to ensure its efficiency.

Both farms had dairy herds and, owing to their proximity and the connection between the families, may have been run in conjunction with one another.

59 NETHERHILLS, FROMEBRIDGE – undated

Netherhills Farm

The farmhouse possibly has a late 17th-century core, which was then altered and enlarged in the 19th century.

Susannah Goatman

By the time of this sketch Susannah Goatman (*c.*1791–1877), from Yatton Keynell, Wiltshire, had been widowed twice having first been married to William Browning and then Richard Goatman. Susannah and William probably came to Netherhills between 1817 and 1819 and when he died in 1822 she was the mother of five children under the age of 10 years. Richard Goatman appears to have lived on the farm from 1828 (or earlier),

NETHERHILLS FARM,
FRAMPTON-ON-SEVERN.

Prime Fat and Store Stock.

BRUTON and KNOWLES

Have received instructions from MR. THOMAS BROWNING

TO SELL BY AUCTION,

Upon the PREMISES on Tuesday, the 26th Feb. 1867, commencing at One o'clock in the afternoon,—

13 Choice FAT COWS and HEIFERS,
3 Fresh BARREN HEIFERS,
1 Well-bred Two-year-old STIRK HEIFER,
2 Ditto STEERS,
2 Yearling ditto,
49 Prime Fat CROSS-BRED TEGS, &c.
Luncheon will be provided.

King Street, Gloucester.

Gloucester Journal, 23 February 1867

although he and Susannah did not marry until 1843. Richard died in 1860.

The dairy farm consisted of 170 acres and remained in Susannah's tenancy until her death. The rich pastures of the Severn Vale were particularly suited to dairy farming and, by careful management of the land, heavy crops of grass were cultivated, thereby providing plentiful hay throughout the winter and enabling the production of good cheese to take place almost without interruption. Milking was normally carried out twice a day, in the early morning and late afternoon, and the milkmaid would take her stool and bucket out to the cows in the field or yard. It was then distributed to the neighbourhood either by the milkmaid carrying covered pails on a yoke, or from large tinned churns transported by pony and trap. The making of butter and cheese were skilled tasks done by hand, and much care was taken to ensure the cleanliness of the dairy buildings and the equipment used.

Thomas Browning

Thomas Browning (*c.*1817–83) was the son of Susannah (above). He had farmed at the other farm at Netherhills from about 1841, and there is evidence from the Clifford family archives that Thomas oversaw the running of his mother's farm towards the end of her life. He too was born at Yatton Keynell, as was his wife Esther. Consisting of about 160 acres, the farm employed 4 men and 2 boys together with a dairymaid. Sheep were also kept.

The position of dairymaid demanded high standards of hygiene, for each day she had to skim the milk, clean and scald the milk pans, the separator, the strainer, and the milk buckets, as well as scrub the dairy itself. The floors would be kept cool with cold water. Butter and

WANTED,—A respectable YOUNG PERSON, to assist in a Farm-House where there is a Dairy of 25 Cows.
Apply to Mr. Browning, Netherhills Farm, Frampton-on-Severn, Gloucestershire.

Gloucester Journal, 26 September 1863

Netherhills Farm. Mrs Goatman. *Fromebri*

cheesemaking were other routine tasks that produced yet more utensils and pans to clean. In small farms such as Thomas Browning's the dairymaid was also expected to assist in the farmhouse, helping to prepare meals and wash up afterwards, as well as collecting and sorting eggs.

Like many of the local farmers, Thomas Browning was supportive of the local community and on a number of occasions was a Guardian or Overseer of the Poor.

60 FROMEBRIDGE – undated

Fromebridge Mill

There has been a mill on this site since the Domesday Book, although the building depicted was rebuilt in the late 18th century and probably extended during the mid-19th century. The millowner's house possibly has a 17th-century core and was enlarged in both the 18th and 19th centuries.

Uriah Godsell

Throughout the 1860s Uriah Godsell was the miller at Fromebridge Mill. The majority of the workers lived in Fromebridge and Godsell seemed keen to subscribe to their welfare by financially supporting the National School in Frampton which some of older children attended. He probably also helped to fund the Infant School in Fromebridge run by Mrs. Park (see page 138). When the poor needed coal in the winter Uriah Godsell gave money to help pay for it.

Born *c.*1827 in Wotton-under-Edge, he married Ann, originally from Whitminster. Their son was born in Illinois, America in 1852, and their daughters in Frampton and Whitminster at a later date.

Mr. Browning's Farm.

FRAMPTON-ON-SEVERN. — *Shocking Accident.* — Yester-
~~y~~ week a fatal accident occurred at Froom-bridge Mills to a boy
~~~ned~~ Moreby, about eight years old, son of Mr. Godsell's miller.
appears that the deceased and some other children were playing
~~ar~~ the water-wheel, when the deceased attempted to cross a plank
framework, underneath which was a grating for the purpose of
~~eping~~ back any obstruction to the undershot water-wheel, which is
~~~ery~~ powerful one, when he slipped, and falling on the water-wheel
~~~o~~, the current soon carried him into the wheel; an alarm was in-
~~~antly~~ raised by the children, the wheel was stopped, and the father
the deceased, with others, ran to the rescue, but too late, as the
~~~heel~~ had passed him, and the body was collected in a shockingly
~~~utilated~~ state. It appears that the framework of the wheel is
~~~arded~~ by a rail placed on the wheel side, but the deceased, child-
~~~e~~, attempted to pass under at the further end.

Gloucester Journal, 4 August 1860

Another unfortunate incident occurred in 1864 involving one of Uriah Godsell's horses after which he was summoned before magistrates on a charge of cruelty. His waggoner, a local from Fromebridge named Worthy King, had taken 120 bushels of beans to Gloucester and was returning with 100 bushels of wheat when he was stopped in Bristol Road, Gloucester, by an officer of the Royal Society for the Prevention of Cruelty to Animals, who had noticed that one of the four horses was pulling differently to the rest. Closer inspection revealed several sores on the horse's shoulders and King was ordered to take the beast from the team and place it behind. A police officer and a local magistrate were both passing the incident and considered the animal to be in a most wretched state.

Godsell failed to put up much of a defence at the trial and was fined £2 including costs. King, who was considered in no way to blame having acted upon the instructions of his master to use the horse, was acquitted. A friend of Godsell's wrote to the *Gloucester Journal* claiming that the horse was in good health and fit for work, but the accompanying veterinary surgeon's certificate had been issued some four weeks after the original incident. A week later the *Gloucester Journal* published a letter from the RSPCA's officer pointing out that the sores could well have healed in that time and wondering why the sworn oaths of a police officer and a

Mr Godsell's Mill ? Froombridge

magistrate were being called into question. So far as the *Gloucester Journal* was concerned the debate had raged long enough, for the editor requested that correspondence be closed on the subject, both sides having been fully heard. No doubt Uriah Godsell suffered a degree of public embarrassment over the matter which must have been the talk of the little hamlet of Fromebridge at the time.

When he died in 1878, Uriah Godsell bequeathed in his will that his wife should have all his household goods including plate and china etc., but that she should not be responsible for any damage or loss during its proper use. He left an estate of almost £25,000, which in today's terms is nearly £1 million. Where Uriah Godsell's wealth came from is not clear, but he certainly would not have made it all from his enterprise at Fromebridge.

Enoch Davis

Enoch Davis (*c*.1824-94) was born in Whitminster. He was the son of Samuel and Sarah Davis (see sketch 61). Enoch and his wife Letitia (who came from Bristol) had eight children of whom three died whilst young.

Enoch was variously an agricultural labourer, fruit dealer and hurdle maker. Hurdles were used about the farms to mend gaps in hedges, for penning sheep and smaller livestock and also as temporary fencing to limit grazing. Enoch Davis would have woven withies or hazel twigs into a sturdy framework of hazel or ash poles. Working from the crack of dawn he could have made as many as twelve hurdles per day. He would have had a good supply of withies from the beds of osiers (a variety of willow) growing along the low-lying streams and drainage ditches in the area.

Davis. Trigg. Hunt. Cartwright. Mrs Park's Infant School

Joseph Trigg

Joseph Trigg (*c*.1793-1870) from Moreton Valence would probably have worked at one of the farms in Fromebridge, along with some of his sons. Joseph was married twice, firstly to Comfort and later Hester. The family had lived in Fromebridge from *c*.1841 and comprised many children, one of which was William (see sketch 61). In 1858 a daughter was baptised twice within the space of a month indicating that she may have been rather sickly at birth. However, as her mother Hester was not present on the second occasion and she was given an additional Christian name (Emily Amelia) by the sponsors, there may have been some family dispute about the naming of the child. Hester Trigg died in 1861 aged 46.

William Hunt

William Hunt was born in Cherington, a village near Minchinhampton, and was probably baptised in 1792. Some mystery surrounds his early life for the County Gaol Registers and *Gloucester Journal* report on a William Hunt born in Cherington but living in Frampton charged with stealing four pigs in 1818. As no trace has been found of any other William Hunt born in Cherington at that time, it is likely that the miscreant was the same man. The sentence he received was Transportation for seven years, but there is no evidence of William leaving the country. He may have appealed against the sentence and had it commuted. The Gaol Registers gave detailed descriptions of the prisoners in order to facilitate identification. The William Hunt which featured in them had brown hair, rather inclined to sandy, with a fair complexion, light brown eyes, flat face, wide mouth, a straight nose and sandy beard. He had a mole on the small of his back and another on his left buttock. His right leg was smaller than the left and there was a small substance under his left ham. He was 5ft. 6in. tall and could read a little.

William was an agricultural labourer/carter. He and his wife Elizabeth (known as Betty) had at least five children. A rather sad incident occurred towards the end of his life, four years before he died (see right).

Gloucester Chronicle, 1 May 1869

Cartwright

It has not been possible to identify the occupants of this house. John Cartwright (senior) was dead by the time the sketch was drawn and John Cartwright (junior) was living on the Bristol Road.

Mrs. Park's Infant School (now The Loft)

Jesse Park (*c*.1803-72) was a woollen weaver who came to Fromebridge in the mid-1830s. He and his wife Mary Ann were both born in Uley. Despite his wife being a schoolmistress, various people had difficulty in spelling both Jesse's Christian name and surname, which appear in many different forms.

Mary Ann Park (or Parks) had managed the little 'Dame School' in Fromebridge for some 30 years prior to her death in 1875. She provided the younger children with an education before, hopefully, they transferred to the National School in Frampton, if their families could spare the money and do without their help at home or in the fields. It was a long walk from Fromebridge to the National School at the far end of Frampton, a distance of some two miles, too far for the infants to travel, so Mrs. Park's Infant School was an important feature of life in the hamlet of Fromebridge. The cost of running the school was very low, with a typical account being the one given in the parish magazine of 1868:

FROOMEBRIDGE SCHOOL.	£	s.	d.		£	s.	d.
Mrs. H. Clifford	2	0	0	Salary	8	0	0
Mr. Bengough	1	0	0	Toward Coals	0	11	7
The Vicar	1	0	0				
Mrs. Goatman	0	10	0				
Mr. Browning	0	5	0				
School Pence	3	16	7				
	£8	11	7		£8	11	7

Mary Ann Park's kitchen was used for evening lectures given by the vicar to the people of Fromebridge 'among whom she had ever shown an example of Christian Piety and resignation'.

61 FROMEBRIDGE, possibly part of Fromebridge Row and the Bristol Road
– undated

William Trigg

William Trigg (*c*.1823-1907) was born at Whitminster. After he married Eliza they had 15 children, 12 of whom were living in this house on the 1871 census with ages ranging from 21

Trigg & Davis. T. Hunt. Davis. T. Cartwright.

downwards to three months. The Triggs appear to have been a close-knit family with several of the children still living at home well into their twenties. William was an agricultural labourer and carter and most of the boys were labourers too. Two of the daughters were later described as 'cloth factory girls'. All the children appear to have been educated to about the age of ten.

Young families such as the Triggs would have enjoyed the visit of a large travelling menagerie, which was exhibited on the village green in July 1865. The collection of wild animals was described as 'really good' and afforded instruction as well as entertainment to a large number of visitors.

Samuel Davis

Samuel Davis (*c.*1797–1885), an agricultural labourer and hurdle maker from Whitminster, married Sarah from Eastington, where their older children were born. The Davis family appear to have come to Fromebridge in about 1841. They were unable to read or write, but it is likely that Samuel and Sarah attended church and listened carefully to Bible stories for many of their children were named after its characters: Joseph, Thomas, Enoch, Hephzibah, Samson, Martha, Samuel, Sarah and Esther. The Davis family were typical of those living in Fromebridge with some of the sons following their father by also becoming agricultural labourers, the daughters being variously employed at the mill or as servants. One was a dressmaker. After the children had left home there was room for Samuel and Sarah to take in lodgers, who generally worked at the mill.

In 1864 the apparently quiet life of Samuel Davis was disturbed when a stranger in Fromebridge asked him the way to Stonehouse:

Gloucester Journal, 16 July 1864

Timothy Hunt

Timothy Hunt (*c.*1829-65) was a carter, born in Eastington. The son of William and Elizabeth Hunt (see sketch 60), in 1851 he was living with both his parents and his future wife, Harriet Smith. Her family had probably come from Uley when her father, a cloth worker, seems to have come to work at Fromebridge Mill. When Timothy and Harriet married later that year, neither of them could write their names. Their two children were baptised in 1861 and 1864 but tragedy struck the family the following year:

Gloucester Journal, 28 October 1865

Samuel Davis

Samuel Davis, variously described as being from Frampton or Eastington, was born *c.*1837, the son of Samuel and Sarah Davis (see above). He was an agricultural labourer and in 1861 his wife Emma was a wool picker, which meant that she removed the burrs from the wool.

Their children probably attended Mrs. Park's Infant School at Fromebridge before moving up to the National School. Early in February 1869 they would have undoubtedly been affected by the very wet and stormy weather that had caused the River Severn to rise to reportedly its highest level for 24 or 25 years. Several roads and meadows in the district were flooded, making travel difficult and preventing the children from attending school.

The Walk Farm. Parker. *Whitminster Lane*

Bristol Road

John Cartwright

John Cartwright (*c*.1805-84), and his father before him, lived in this house on the Bristol Road, near to Fromebridge. John was a labourer working on the roads, the land or anything else that brought him employment. Money was tight in families such as that of John and Hannah Cartwright, and the children were lucky if they received much education. One son aged seven was admitted to the lowest class of the National School in 1863, 'being able to read fairly in monosyllables; could not write', and another was at work by the age of ten.

62   WALK FARM, WHITMINSTER LANE – undated

The farmhouse was probably built in the 17th century. It was cased in brick and enlarged in the 19th century.

John Parker

According to the Registers of Electors, John Parker was at Walk Farm as occupier of the land from before 1859-60 (some earlier books are missing) until 1882. He had been born in Coaley *c*.1831.

   On the 1861 census he was employing eight labourers, two women and two boys, unmarried, with his sister Elizabeth who was presumably running the house for him. During the next decade his workforce reduced to three labourers and three boys and by 1881, following changes in the law concerning the employment of children John Parker's employees had dropped still further to three labourers and one boy. Although horse-drawn mechanical reapers

came in from about the 1850s they were for a long time supplementary to hand labour and most of the corn was still cut by scythe, sickle or bagging hook. It was slow, laborious work and a gang of five men would require a day to cut two acres.

John Parker married Amelia Susanna Camm of Coaley in 1862, and in common with many farmers, he chose to employ a governess to help educate his children. The employment of a 13-year-old nursemaid in 1871 indicates just how young some of the local girls were when they entered into responsible jobs.

63   THE LAKE – 23 August 1866

Richard Knight-Wright

Richard Knight-Wright (*c*.1808-85), a brickmaker and layer, was born in Frampton the son of Richard Wright and wife Ann (née Knight). Richard had at least six children by his first wife Mary, and the family lived in various cottages around the village. Richard Knight-Wright came to live in Lake Cottage between 1851 and 1861 with his second wife Ann, who was a laundress.

Andrews

This probably refers to George Andrews (*c*.1835-1925), a carpenter who worked, certainly in later life, on ships. Born in Hardwicke, George was the son of Joseph Andrews, a blacksmith, who lived on the northern edge of The Green. He married Mary Burford Daniels in 1860 at St Mary's Church and they lived in Frampton for a number of years before moving for a short while to Fretherne. During the mid-1860s Mary Andrews worked for Thomas Karn at the *Bell Inn*.

George Wright

George Wright (*c*.1831-89), a waterman from Whitminster, and his young family lived at The Lake from the very late 1850s. His wife Caroline was a laundress who originated from Hardwicke. He evidently got more than a little merry on Boxing Day in 1860 and was fined 5s. (and 4s. 6d. costs) for being drunk and for fighting at Whitminster according to a report in the *Gloucester Chronicle*.

G. Knight

There were several families called Knight living in Frampton during the 1860s and this property was probably occupied by George and Elizabeth Knight and their children. Elizabeth was a daughter of Giles Frape, the parish clerk. George was a shipwright, and the early years after their marriage in 1856 had been spent in Gloucester. Between *c*.1865 and 1870 he seems to have been in partnership with Frederick Evans of Saul, building ships at their yard at the Sandfield Bridge, on the canal just north of the parish of Frampton in neighbouring Saul. One son, Garibaldi, took to playing truant from the National School on a regular basis despite the best efforts of Mrs. Gleed, the sewing mistress, who happened to be his aunt. The Knights returned to Gloucester in 1870.

Thomas Hobbs

Thomas Hobbs (*c*.1840-1900), a carpenter originally from Westbury-on-Severn, owned this property at The Lake where he lived with his wife Mary Elizabeth. They had come to Frampton shortly before the sketch was drawn and several of their children were born in the village.

Lake House

William Monday

Following the Highway Act of 1862 parishes were united to form Highway Districts and in 1863 William Monday was appointed District Surveyor.

The Wheatenhurst Highway District comprised the parishes of Arlingham, Eastington, Frampton, Fretherne, Frocester, Hardwicke, Haresfield, Kings Stanley, Leonard Stanley, Longney, Moreton Valence, Quedgeley, Randwick, Saul, Standish, Stonehouse and Wheatenhurst. Several roads in the area were worked upon during William Monday's time in charge and advertisements for the supply and delivery of suitable stone regularly appeared in the *Gloucester Journal*. However, the job of District Road Surveyor not only

To Road Surveyors.
WHEATENHURST HIGHWAY DISTRICT.

NOTICE is hereby given, that the next MEETING of the WHEATENHURST HIGHWAY BOARD will be held, pursuant to adjournment, at Whitminster Inn, in the Parish of Wheatenhurst, on Monday, the 20th of April instant, at eleven o'clock, for the purpose of APPOINTING A DISTRICT SURVEYOR. Salary, £100 a year. Surveyor to devote his whole time to the office; to keep a horse, and reside in some central part of the District to be approved by the Board. Two sureties in £100 each, to the satisfaction of the Board, will be required. It is desirable that Candidates should attend the Meeting.

Applications in the handwriting of the Candidate, with testimonials as to character and ability, to be sent to the Clerk to the said Board, on or before Thursday, the 16th instant,

JOHN VIZARD,
Clerk to the said Highway Board.
Dursley, 2nd April, 1863.

Gloucester Journal, 4 April 1863

concerned him in matters of the upkeep of the roads; he also made sure that they were not being unlawfully blocked. In 1866 a case was heard at Whitminster Petty Sessions in which Thomas Halsey, a farmer from Whitminster, was accused of placing 20 loads of manure within seven feet of the centre of the highway. The defendant argued that manure had been left in the same place for the last forty years. Nevertheless he was fined one shilling, with four shillings costs and instructed to remove the manure.

William and Eliza Monday lived in Lake House between 1864 and 1867, having come from Whitminster. The property comprised three parlours, seven private bedrooms, the 'requisite domestic offices' and a plentiful supply of very pure water. The garden and lawn were described as large. It is possible that William and Eliza Monday did not use the whole of the property for themselves as there was an advertisement in the *Gloucester Journal* in 1865 giving details of furnished or unfurnished apartments to let at Lake House.

The Mondays' elder children had been privately educated before coming to Frampton, but they soon settled into life at the National School. One rather unusual incident involving them was described in the logbook: 'Oct. 26th 1863 – Jane Monday had her hand very badly cut this morning accidentally. She was playfully striking her brother and hit a knife he was using'.

The Denhalls (now Wisma Mulia)

The Denhalls is not featured in the sketches as the house was situated in Saul, just outside the parish boundary of the 1860s. Nowadays the property, located just to the south of Bridge Road between the Bell Inn and the Gloucester and Sharpness Canal, is much altered and known as Wisma Mulia.

Thomas Watts

During the early 1860s Thomas Watts (*c*.1822-92), the local surgeon, moved to The Denhalls with his wife Lucy and their young children. Thomas had become a Member of the Royal College of Surgeons and a Licentiate of the Society of Apothecaries of London in 1844 before assisting his father, also Thomas, as surgeon in Frampton. When Thomas Watts senior died in 1855, Thomas junior was his natural successor. The Watts were a much respected family in the village and were thoroughly involved in the welfare of its people. His mother Ann and sisters Elizabeth and Anne lived at The Grange.

Thomas' duties were those of General Practitioner to the people of the village and surrounding area. He was called upon to perform minor operations and attend childbirths as well as administering inoculations against such diseases as smallpox. In the 1860s the village almost escaped the most feared disease of all, cholera; just one case being reported and cured in 1865. In the same year Thomas Watts also successfully treated a patient with yellow fever. Often he would carry out postmortem and attend inquests when an unexpected or suspicious death occurred. His evidence was crucial as was seen in the case of Mary Humberstone, tried for the manslaughter of Elizabeth Webb (see sketch 15), where he indicated that death was from the passion of their argument rather than from the blow struck to Elizabeth Webb's head by a fire shovel, and Mary Humberstone was only convicted of an assault charge.

Dr. Watts contacted the National School on one occasion in 1863 to report that he had seen a pupil who had contracted 'the itch' (scabies). This resulted in his examining all 87 children the next day, finding just one case.

As a doctor Thomas Watts was ever mindful of the safety of his patients, and at a time when farm accidents were all too common, and often fatal, he was well aware of the dangers of the new machinery that was gradually being introduced into the village.

In the 1860s Thomas Watts was assisted first by Alfred John Gulliver Waters and later Hampden Bernard Wotton. Alfred Waters shared Thomas Watts' interest in local enterprise and both were very active supporters of the Literary and Mechanics' Institute. Waters in particular was a great organiser, finding time, as Honorary Secretary of the Frampton and Fretherne Cottage Gardeners' Society, to run their first three annual shows from 1863-5.

Thomas Watts longed for a son and heir, having only daughters, and when Lucy finally bore him Thomas Henry Evered Watts in 1872 the villagers were so anxious to join with them in their celebrations that a peal of bells was rung. In return, as was the custom, Lucy Watts provided the ringers with a supper a few days later.

WHITMINSTER PETTY SESSIONS, *Thursday.*— (Before H. H. Wilton, J. A. G. Clarke, E. G. Ll. Baker, Esqrs. and the Rev. T. Peters.)—*John Cole,* a labourer in the employ of Mr. Benjamin Hill, of Packthorn Farm, was summoned for having, on the 28th ult. erected a steam-engine within 25 yards of the public road at Frampton-on-Severn, the engine not being placed in any barn or building, or behind any wall or fence sufficient to screen it from the road.

Mr. Hill, the owner of the engine, said the defendant was in the Militia, and could not attend, and he hoped the Bench would go into the case at once, and he should admit the offence.

Dr. T. Watts, of Frampton, the complainant, deposed that the steam thrashing machine and engine were placed close to the high road, so as to be very dangerous to persons riding or driving by, and he had instituted these proceedings to show people that such a practice was illegal. The engine was at work when he passed it. His object was to make known through the county that these engines could not be worked within 25 yards of any road.

The Bench said it was a most dangerous practice to work engines in this way. The law said that any person working a steam engine within 25 yards of any road or highway, and not in any house, or behind any fence, was liable to a penalty of 5l. This being the first offence, defendant was fined 1s. and 8s. costs. They remarked that if he or any other person was convicted for a similar offence, they should impose a heavier penalty.

Mr. Hill paid the fine and costs.

Gloucester Journal, 8 May 1868

Conclusion

With its wealth of activities and characters, Frampton on Severn was, no doubt, similar to many other villages in the 1860s. The gentry and poor, craftsmen and labourers, living side by side and helping each other out in times of need, formed a typical English rural community. The detailed picture that I have been able to build up has been helped immensely by the enormous number of records available and I am grateful to everyone, past and present, who has thoughtfully preserved those documents. May I urge you all to deposit whatever records you can with your local Record Office so that they can be kept properly and safely for the generations to come.

Sources and Further Reading

PRIMARY SOURCES

Atkyns, Sir Robert, *The Ancient and Present State of Gloucestershire* (1712, reprinted 1974)

Bigland, Ralph (ed. Frith, Brian), *Historical, Monumental and Genealogical Collections Relative to the County of Gloucester* (1990)

Census Returns (1841-1891)

Clifford family Archives

The Compleat Parish Office, 7th edn. (1734, reprinted 1996)

Gloucester Chronicle

Gloucester Journal

Hockaday Abstracts

Holdsworth, W.A., *The Handy Book of Parish Law* (1859 reprinted 1995)

Hurley, Beryl (ed.), *The Book of Trades or Library of Useful Arts*, 4th edn. (1811, reprinted 1993)

Inclosure Map of Frampton on Severn (1815), reproduced by Geoff Gwatkin (1998)

Michell, George B., 'The Frampton on Severn Volunteers 1798-1802', *Journal of the Society of Army Historical Research* (1928)

Parish Registers and other Parish Documents

Records of Frampton on Severn Church of England School

Records of Frampton on Severn Congregational Church

Rudder, Samuel, *A New History of Gloucestershire* (1779, reprinted 1977)

Rudge, Thomas, *The History of the County of Gloucestershire* (1803)

SECONDARY SOURCES

Bailey, Jocelyn, *The Village Blacksmith*, 2nd edn. (1998)

Bailey, Jocelyn, *The Village Wheelwright and Carpenter* (1998)

Bédarida, François, *A Social History of England 1851-1975* (1979)

Best, Geoffrey, *Mid-Victorian Britain 1851-75* (1985)

Bettey, J.H., *Church and Parish* (1987)

Blewett, Jean and Crompton, Craig, *Discovering Frampton on Severn* (n.d.)

Bourne, Susan & Chicken, Andrew H., *Records of the Medical Professions* (1994)

Breckon, Bill & Parker, Jeffrey, *Tracing the History of Houses* (1996)

Briggs, Asa, *The Age of Improvement 1783-1867* (1980)

Clifford, Rollo, *The Royal Gloucestershire Hussars* (1991)

Conway-Jones, Hugh, *The Gloucester and Sharpness Canal* (1999)

Dibben, A.A., *Title Deeds*, 2nd edn. (1990)

Elrington, C.R. & Herbert, N.M., *Victoria County History*, vol.10 (1972)

Evans, Eric J. & Crosby, Alan G., *Tithes*, 3rd edn. (1997)

Eveleigh, David J., *Candle Lighting* (1995)

Eveleigh, David J., *The Victorian Farmer* (1996)

Fearn, Jacqueline, *Domestic Bygones* (1987)

Fearn, Jacqueline, *Thatch and Thatching* (1995)

Foster, David, *The Rural Constabulary Act 1839* (1982)

Frampton on Severn Women's Institute, *A Guide Book to Frampton on Severn* (1952)

Hammond, Martin, *Bricks and Brickmaking*, 2nd edn. (1998)

Harvey, Nigel, *Old Farm Buildings*, 3rd edn. (1997)

Hayward, Edward, *Gloucester, Stroud and Berkeley* (1970)

Herbert, Nicholas, *Road, Travel and Transport* (1985)

HMSO, *Nonconformist Chapels and Meeting Houses in Gloucestershire* (1986)

Horn, Pamela, *The Rise and Fall of the Victorian Servant* (1990)

Hoskins, W.G., *Local History in England*, 2nd edn. (1972)

Ingram, Arthur, *Dairying Bygones*, 2nd edn. (1977)

Jackson, W.A., *The Victorian Chemist and Druggist* (1999)

Kilby, K., *The Village Cooper* (1998)

Kissack, Keith, *The River Severn* (1982)

Mabey, Richard, *The Frampton Flora* (1985)

Machin, Bob, *Rural Housing* (1994)

Marcombe, David, *The Victorian Sailor* (1995)

Markwell, F.C. & Saul, Pauline, *The Family Historian's Enquire Within*, 3rd edn. (1988)

May, Trevor, *An Economic and Social History of Britain 1760-1970* (1992)

May, Trevor, *The Victorian Domestic Servant* (1998)

May, Trevor, *The Victorian Schoolroom* (1998)

May, Trevor, *The Victorian Undertaker* (1996)

May, Trevor, *The Victorian Workhouse* (1999)

McLaughlin, Eve, *Annals of the Poor*, 5th edn. (1994)

McLaughlin, Eve, *Illegitimacy*, 6th edn. (1995)

McLaughlin, Eve, *Nonconformist Ancestors* (1995)

McLaughlin, Eve, *The Poor are always with us* (1994)

Meadows, Cecil A., *The Victorian Ironmonger*, 2nd edn. (1997)

Michell, George B., *Frampton on Severn* (1928)

Mills, Stephen & Reimer, Pierce, *The Mills of Gloucestershire* (1989)

Milward, Rosemary, *A Glossary of Household, Farming and Trade Terms from Probate Inventories*, 3rd edn. (1993)

Mingay, G.E., *Rural Life in Victorian England* (1998)

Morris, Christopher, *Dairy Farming in Gloucestershire* (1983)

Mote, Gordon, *The Westcountrymen* (1986)

Muller, H.G., *Baking and Bakeries* (1986)

Munby, Lionel, *How much is that worth?*, 2nd edn. (1996)

Oldacre, Susan, *A Blacksmith's Daughter* (1985)

Palgrave-Moore, Patrick, *How to locate and use Manorial Records* (1985)

Powell, Christopher, *Discovering Cottage Architecture* (1996)

Richardson, John, *The Local Historian's Encyclopedia*, 2nd edn. (1989)

Sambrook, Pamela, *Laundry Bygones* (1997)

Saville, Alan, *Archaeology in Gloucestershire* (1984)

Simpson, Elizabeth (comp.), *Latin Word-List for Family Historians* (1985)

Smith, A.H., *Placenames of Gloucestershire*, vol.2 (1964)

Smith, D.J., *Discovering Country Crafts*, 2nd edn. (1980)

Smith, D.J., *Discovering Horse Drawn Carriages* (1974)

Smith, Michael S., *Frampton on Severn: A Brief History* (1986)

Sparkes, Ivan G., *Four-poster and Tester Beds* (1990)

Staniforth, Arthur, *Straw and Straw Craftsmen*, 2nd edn. (1991)

Stroud District Council, *Frampton on Severn: Local Plan and Conservation Area* (1976)

Stroud District Council, *Frampton on Severn: Adopted Local Plan and Conservation Area* (1977)

Sutton, Alan, *The Severn Vale in Old Photographs* (1986)

Swann, June, *Shoemaking* (1997)

Tann, Jennifer, *Gloucestershire Woollen Mills* (1967)

Various Trade Directories including *Pigot & Co.* (1830 & 1844), *Hunt & Co.* (1847), *Morris & Co.* (1865-6), *Slater's* (1868)

Verey, David, *Gloucestershire: The Vale and the Forest of Dean*, 2nd edn. (1998)

Vince, John, *Mills and Millwrighting* (1978)

Vince, John, *The Village School* (1993)

Waters, Brian, *Severn Tide* (1947)

Whiting, J.R.S., 'The Frampton Volunteers', *Gloucestershire Historical Studies* (1967)

Willis, Margaret, *The Ferry between Newnham and Arlingham* (1993)

Wiltshire, Lewis, *The Vale of Berkeley* (1980)

Wyatt, Irene (ed.), *Transportees from Gloucester to Australia 1783-1842* (1988)

I would also like to acknowledge the help of many private individuals who shared their research and findings with me, together with the following repositories:

Cheltenham Reference Library

Dr. Williams's Library, London

Gloucester Local Studies Library

Gloucester Reference Library

Gloucestershire Record Office

Gloucestershire Register Office

National Monuments Record Centre, Swindon

Northamptonshire Record Office

Somerset Record Office

Up Hatherley Library, Cheltenham

Wiltshire Record Office

Index

Ad Extremum, 44
Advowson Farm, 37, 38, 121
Advowsons, 37
agricultural implement/machine maker, 39, 40
agricultural labourer, 20, 25, 37, 41, 56, 59, 60, 61, 69, 71, 72, 73, 78, 79, 81, 82, 84, 92, 94, 96, 107, 112, 117, 126, 127, 136, 138, 139, 140
Alder, 99-101
Aldridge, 76, 91, 94-5
Allen, 26, 49, 52-3, 84, 104, 112
allotment, 23, 69, 117
Amberley Cottage, 76
Andrews, 21, 142-3
apprentice, 19, 27, 35, 40, 63, 64, 114, 127
attorney, 12
auction, 12, 14, 18, 19, 30, 39, 48, 72, 84, 103, 128, 133
Ayland, 47, 58, 101

bacon curer, 46
bailiff, 128
baker, 30, 77, 112, 121
bakery, 38, 41, 112, 121
Ballinger, 40, 41, 45, 112
band, 46, 66, 104
barber, 117
barge owner, 29, 44, 63, 72, 81, 116
bargeman, 60
Barnard, 65, 72, 81, 84, 120
Barnett, 112
Barnsdale, 123
Barradell, 20, 69-70
Barrett, 14-15
bazaar, 65, 99
Beehive Academy, 116
Beehive Cottage, 58, 106
beer retailer/seller, 46, 76, 98, 117
beerhouse/beershop, 53, 97, 98, 103, 121
Bell Inn, 11, 18-19, 20, 30, 42, 48, 84, 103, 107, 128, 143
bell ringers, 93, 145
bells, 66, 93, 115, 119, 145
Bendles, 59
Bengough, 138
Bennett, 10-11, 12-13, 33, 35, 45, 125
Bignell, 70, 76, 94
Bird, 31, 32-3, 38
bird keeping, 78
Birt, 68
Bishop, 53
blacksmith, 19, 21, 40, 43, 49, 116, 117, 142
Blenheim House, 113
Bodnum, 76
Bokhara, 50
Bond, 107, 108
boot and shoemaker; see shoemaker
Bosworth, 81
Brabazon, 76
Brazenton/Brazington, 37-8, 59
brick and tile maker, 81

bricklayer, 59, 60, 69, 71, 75, 83, 88, 93, 96, 99, 126, 142
brickmaker, 96, 112, 142
brickpit, 54
brickyard, 54, 83, 95
brickyard woman, 83
bridgekeeper, 86, 87
Brinkworth, 110
Bristol Channel, 29, 58, 63
Bristol Road, 138, 141
British School, 30, 122
Brook House, 115, 116
Brooklyn, 55
Brooks, 60, 82, 83
Brown, 61
Browning, 25, 78, 82, 130, 133-4, 138
Bubb, 65, 72, 121, 129-131
Buckholdt, 52, 53, 54, 55, 116
Buckholdt Cottages, 51, 53, 112
Buckle Brook, 53
Buckle-bridge House, 53
builder, 50, 60, 69, 99, 105, 125, 126
Burman, 50, 107
Burr, 49, 51, 52, 67, 104, 118, 120
butcher, 27, 40, 46, 56, 63, 67, 111, 118, 119, 122, 126
butler, 8
Byrne, 62

cabinet maker, 31, 51, 103, 118
Camm, 142
candlemaking, 44-5
Cant Leaze, 124
Caple, 77
captain, 29, 31
Cardiff House, 30, 35, 106, 110
carpenter and wheelwright, 14, 19, 32, 41, 47, 49, 50, 52, 106, 108, 109, 118, 123, 142, 143
carrier, 45, 82, 117
carter, 25, 81, 82, 86, 94, 126, 132, 138, 139, 140
Carter, 98, 116
Cartwright, 138, 141
Catechism, 64, 121-2
Causon, 69
census enumerator, 10, 38, 52, 57, 71, 79, 92, 127
Chapel House, 122
Chapel/Congregational School, 33, 41, 66, 82, 112, 116
Chapman, 22
Chappell, 52
Charles, 43, 58, 72
Charles II, 69
charwoman, 31, 79, 117
chemist and druggist, 11, 76
child labour, 65, 72-3, 85, 141
chimney sweep, 140
choir, 66, 90, 99
cholera, 144
choristers, 90
Church Court, 71, 73, 91, 92, 94, 95
Church Court Cottage, 92, 93
Church End, 93, 94, 95, 101
Church End Cottage, 91, 92

Church End House, 80, 81, 82
Church Farm, 19, 54, 93, 101, 102
Church Lane, 88
Church of England Temperance Society, 28, 75
church practice, 37
church seating, 59
Churchside Cottage, 92
churchwarden, 15, 54, 88, 91, 100, 132
churchyard, 17, 23, 41, 52, 91, 93, 117
Chute, 89
Clarence House, 116
Clarke, 18, 37, 39, 41, 80, 112
Clegg, 116, 124
Click, 88
Clifford, 7-9, 14, 15, 18, 19, 21-4, 25, 29, 30, 34, 41, 46, 54, 56, 58, 59, 65, 69, 73, 74, 77, 78, 81, 83, 85, 88, 94, 97, 99, 100, 101, 103, 104, 105, 117, 126, 128, 129, 138; see also Fair Rosamund
cloth, 50, 132, 139, 140
clothing club, 37
Clutterbuck, 47, 140
Coach House, The, 76
coal merchant, 30, 63, 81
coals, 7, 24, 37, 130, 134
coffee house, 27
Cole, 60, 73, 92, 145
Collector of Taxes, 81
Collett, 60
Collingwood Terrace, 117
Combe Cottage, 95
communion plate, 91
concert, 31, 56, 65, 66, 74, 90, 99, 113, 115
Congregational Chapel/Church, 16, 75, 116, 118, 123-4
cook, 24, 36, 74
Cook/Cooke, 44, 97
Coole, 40-1, 43, 46, 67, 92, 116-17, 119
cooper, 34
Cooper, 58-9
corporal punishment, 63
Cother, Mr., 31
coursing, 63, 132
Cowley, 76
cowman, 27
cricket, 127
curate, 21, 89

dairymaid, 131, 133, 134
Dame School at Fromebridge; see Fromebridge School
Daniels, 142
Darell, 13
Davies/Davis, 15, 49, 132, 136, 139, 140
Daw, 58, 60, 68, 71, 72
De Lacy Cottage, 46
De Lacy Hall, 46
De Mallett, 46
deacon, 50, 81, 124
dealer, 33

Dean, 55
decorator, 115
Denfurlong Cottage, 78
Denfurlong Farm, 27, 80
Denhalls, The, 144
District Road Surveyor, 143
doctor, 9, 42, 66, 144
Dodd, 112, 116
Dodwell, 118
domestic service, 50
Dopping, 77
Doppings House, 77
Dowdeswell, 44, 45, 48, 106
draper; see grocer and draper
Draper, 25, 26, 27, 108, 126
dressmaker, 52, 55, 105, 139
Druid, 63, 72
Dunn, 42, 53, 110-12
Dunsford, 89

earthquake, 43
Eddolls, 8, 102
electricity, 96
Elm Tree Cottage, 19
Emerson, 62
errand boy, 82
Evans, 41-2, 49-50, 57, 68, 80, 85, 95, 97, 99, 104, 109, 112, 143

Fair Rosamund Clifford, 14
Falfield Cottage, 50, 106, 107
farm, 14, 36, 39, 50, 80, 100, 101, 102, 129, 132, 133
farm labourer; see agricultural labourer
farmer, 14, 15, 19, 23, 27, 36, 48, 64, 65, 69, 80, 86, 111, 121, 128, 130, 131, 134, 142, 144
farrier, 40
Fern Cottage, 72
Ferndale, 98
Fernleigh, 40
Ferns, The, 72
fête, 8, 100
Field Farm, 82, 84
fire, 8, 70, 78, 81, 132, 138
fire engine, 8, 132
fireworks, 67
Firs, The, 34
fishing, 87
fishing trade, 46
Fitcherbury, 20, 25, 26, 123
football, 127
footman, 8, 24
foot-race, 117, 119
Ford, 41, 112
Forster's Education Act 1870, 65
Frampton and Fretherne Cottage Gardeners' Society, 13, 26, 52, 61, 69, 119, 145
Frampton Choral Union, 90
Frampton Cottage, 21, 22
Frampton Court, 7, 8, 9, 21, 22, 24, 27, 34, 66, 69, 70, 88, 100, 125, 126, 127
Frampton Farm, 14
Frampton Fat Cattle Fair, 36, 128
Frampton Feast, 44, 74
Frampton Lodge, 21, 22, 24

Frampton on Severn Friendly Society, 107
Frampton Sailing Club, 37
Frampton Vessel Owners' Insurance Club, 52, 58
Frampton Volunteers, 103-4
Frape, 93, 124, 143
Fredericks, 48
French, 54, 93, 94, 101-2
French polisher, 55
Fretherne Court, 13
Friends, 63, 72
Fromebridge, 21, 65, 89, 111, 132-41
Fromebridge Mill, 132, 134, 135, 139, 140
Fromebridge Row, 138
Fromebridge School, 24, 138
fruit dealer/grower, fruiter, 117, 136
Fryer, 28
fundholder, 105

Gabb, 33
gamekeeper, 25, 46, 82, 128
gardener, 8, 13, 41, 61, 69, 84, 88, 93, 94, 96, 108, 117, 119, 126
Gardner, 33
George Hotel, Frocester, 20, 33, 48
Gerrish, 56
Gibbs, 58
glass and china, 106
glazier, 15
Gleed, 93, 143
Gloucester and Berkeley Canal, 14, 29, 30, 54, 63, 69, 81, 84, 86, 95, 109, 143
Gloucester Artillery and Engineers' Band, 13
Gloucester Cattle Market, 80, 101
Gloucester Infirmary, 31, 74, 138
Gloucester Wagon Works Band, 107
Goatman, 39-40, 61-2, 133, 138
Godfrey, 10
Godsell, 134, 135, 136
Gould, 43
Goulding, 80, 97
governess, 24, 142
Grange, The, 36, 59, 119, 144
gravedigger, 93
Green, 21
Green House, The, 9, 70
Green, The, 36, 67, 127, 139
greengrocer, 33
Greening, 37, 38
Grey, 42
Greycroft, 26, 107, 108
Griffin, 8, 93, 132
grocer and draper, 17, 30, 106, 114, 116
groom, 36, 75, 124
Guardian of the Poor, 81, 130, 134
Gully, 68
Gun Powder Plot Day, 96
Guy, 56, 60, 67, 71, 78, 92, 105

Hadley, 47, 48
Hadley's Farm, 35, 36
Hadley's Piece, 35

Haines, 31, 32
Hairdressers, The, 119
Hale, 31, 32, 33
hallier (haulier), 33, 59, 81, 82, 98
Halsey, 144
Happy-go-Lucky, 58, 72
Harmer, 31
Harper, 47
Harris, 88
Hart, 47, 108, 110
Harts Cottages, 110, 111, 112, 125
harvest, 39, 62, 72-3, 129, 130
Harvest Festival, 119
Harvest Holiday, 64
hawker, 42
Hawker, 49, 96, 98, 108
Hawkins, 40, 95, 98
Hazell, 82, 83
Heart of Oak, 30, 102, 103
Heiron, 56, 67, 100, 101
Henry II, 14
Hewer, 128, 129
Hewlett, 17, 19, 52, 115-16, 117, 118-19, 123
Higgins, 19, 125
Highgrove Farm; *see* Oegrove Farm
Highway Act 1862, 143
Hill, 17, 20, 48, 65, 102, 112, 123, 145
Hitchings, 48, 106-7
Hobbs, 8, 27, 29, 43, 44, 45, 63, 67, 69, 72, 96, 117, 118, 119, 125, 143
Hooper, 14-15, 84, 140
Horner, 12, 120
hounds, 63
housekeeper, 8, 18, 68, 103, 112, 117
housemaid, 8, 24, 27, 36, 74
Hulbert, 28, 65
Humberstone, 42, 144
Hunt, 37-8, 71, 137, 138, 140
hunting, 22
hurdle maker, 136, 139
Hyett, 42

Infant School, 134, 138, 140
infant teacher, 57, 76, 95
Inland Revenue Tax Collector, 35
Inn, The, 102
inquest, 18, 42, 68, 102, 140, 144

Jobbins, 127
Jones, 8, 126

Karn, 14, 18-19, 30, 72, 84, 103, 107, 125, 143
Keatinge, 76
Keeper's Cottage, 26
Kemmett, 94
Kempsey House, 121
King, 35, 76, 121, 135
kitchenmaid, 8
Knight, 79, 83, 121, 142, 143
Knight-Wright, 92, 142

labourer, 26, 31, 32, 37, 38, 43, 53, 59, 60, 63, 70, 78, 82, 86, 92, 94, 100, 101, 117, 129, 130, 132, 139, 141, 145

labourer's clothes, 79
ladies' maid, 74
Lake Cottage, 142
Lake House, 123, 143, 144
Lake, The, 121, 142, 143
Lambourn, 92
Land Tax, 52, 102, 116
Lapwing, The, 87, 109
laundress, 33, 67, 107, 117, 124, 142, 143
laundry, 56
Laurels, The, 99, 126
Lawrence, 72, 79, 124
Leather Bottle Lane, 42
Lewis, 28, 66, 75, 123-4
Leyland, 62
licensed victualler, 110
lieutenant, 22
Literary and Mechanics' Institute, 12, 23, 24, 66, 72, 74, 81, 108, 113, 118, 119-21, 127, 145
Lockey, 77
Lodge, 31, 53, 103-4
lodger, 15, 33, 38, 107, 126, 139
Loft, The, 138
Long, 72
Longney, 69
Longney Lass, 63
lunatic, 51

magistrate, 9, 15, 22, 27, 31, 63, 99, 110, 135
maid, 50
Mallard Cottage, 125
Malthouse Cottage, 50
maltster, 50, 81
Manning, 110
Manor Cottage, 28
Manor Farm, 14
Manor Farm Cottages, 12, 13, 14
manslaughter, 42, 144
marble mason; *see* mason
Marda House, 43
marine, 118
marine store dealer, 43, 92
mariner, 31, 60, 69, 72, 84, 92, 95, 98, 110, 112, 116, 121, 124
market boats, 87
mason, 10, 13, 41, 50, 83, 105
May Pole Day, 69
Mayor of Frampton, 67
measles, 62, 64
Mechanics' Institute; *see* Literary and Mechanics' Institute
menagerie, 139
merchant, 53
Merrett, 47, 78
midshipman, 22
milkmaid, 133
mill; *see* Fromebridge Mill
Millard, 36, 50, 96, 108-9
miller, 134
Mills, 19, 69, 73, 75
minister, 60, 67, 75, 114, 116, 123, 124
Monday, 143-4
monitor, 63, 64, 65
Mop Fair, 85
Moreby, 135
Morgan, 17, 49, 50, 81, 96, 99, 104, 124, 126

Morgan's Little Men, 66
murder, 42
Mylne, 86

Nastfield Cottage, 31, 32
Nastfield Farm, 31, 72, 121, 129
National School, 7, 15, 24, 25, 37, 46, 55, 57, 62, 63, 64-66, 69, 70, 72, 74, 85, 90, 92, 93, 96, 99, 100, 112, 116, 118, 119, 121, 122, 127, 132, 138, 141, 144
Neale, 45, 46-7, 121
needlewoman, 48
needlework, 37, 62, 64
Netherhills, 133, 134
Netherhills Farm, 133
New Grounds, 132
New Inn, The, 98
Newcombe, 48
newspaper errand boy, 82
Niblett, 32
Night School, 66
nonconformist, 16, 17, 97, 122, 123
Northend House, 20
Norwich Union Fire Insurance Society, 8, 10, 12, 81, 99, 132
Nurbury, 61
nurse, 33
nursemaid/nurserymaid, 24, 142

Oegrove Farm, 36, 77, 78
old age pension, 74, 107
Old Bakery, The, 112
Old Coffee House, The, 27
Old Post Office, The, 20, 21
Old School House, 101
Old School House, The, 105
Old Thatch, The, 96, 97
Orangery, 8, 9, 70
Orchard, 44, 45, 48, 106
Orchard House, 76
Order of Removal, 107
organist, 51
ostler (stableman), 20, 30
Overseer of the Poor, 10, 49, 51, 99, 105, 107, 134

painter, 15, 115
Palace, 29
parish clerk, 93, 123, 143
parish constable; *see* police
parish magazine, 11, 17, 32, 74, 113
parish, parochial or poor relief, 48, 51, 67, 78, 130
Park/Parks 26, 134, 138, 140
Park Corner, 71, 72, 73, 82
Park Cottage, 26
Park Lodge, 126
Park, The, 126, 127
Parker, 141-2
Parks Cottage, 31
Parks Farm, 31, 85, 130, 131
parochial relief; *see* parish relief
Parry, 90
pauper, 51, 78, 126
Pelican Assurance, 16
Penny Bank, 24, 74
Perks, 88
Perry, 49
Perry Way, 125, 126, 127
Perry Way Lodge, 8, 126

Perrymead Cottage, 126
Perryway Cottage, 126
pew opener, 93
pews, 52, 118
Phipps, 72
photographic artist, 19
Pick, 20, 30
Pill Farm, 83
plumber, 15, 115
poaching, 128
police, 50, 110, 111
police station, 99
Poole House 125
poor, 24, 40, 54
poor relief; *see* parish relief
pork butcher, 46, 121
Portland Place, 11, 12
Post Office, 13, 35, 74, 106
Post Office Savings Bank, 13, 74
Posting House, 18
postmaster, 13
postmistress, 13
pound, 88
Pound Lane, 88
Powell, 93, 125
Price, 19, 70
Priday, 19, 112, 125
Primrose Cottage, 67, 68
Prince of Wales, 52, 54, 66, 118
private school, 113, 132
proprietor of houses, 10, 105, 125
Prospect Cottage, 40
Providence Cottage, 76
pump, 15, 39
pupil teacher, 30, 62, 63, 64, 65, 96, 119, 127

Rag Mop Alley, 42
railway clerk, 50
Rea, 63, 86-7, 92, 94, 95
Red House, The, 15, 80
Red Scarf Club, 74, 107, 108
registrar, 49, 99
rent, 7, 14, 18, 19, 23, 29, 34, 59, 71, 73, 78, 79, 83, 88, 92, 94, 101, 117
rent dinner, 18
Restaurant on the Green, 114
Richardson, 17, 123
Ricketts, 117-18
Ridgwood, 125
rinderpest, 80
River Severn, 14, 29, 63, 68, 140
Roberts, 94
Roe's Pool House, 121, 122, 124
Roseleigh, 98
Rowles, 53-4, 65, 103, 114, 116
Royal Gloucestershire Regiment of Hussar Yeomanry, 22
Royal Society for the Prevention of Cruelty to Animals, 135
Rudder, 123
Runton Cottage, 118
Rural Constabulary Act 1839, 111
Russell, 16, 30, 48, 65
Russell House, 16

sailor, 70
St John, 14, 17, 40, 73-5, 76, 89, 91, 93, 118, 124

St Mary's Church, 15, 54, 66, 88-91
Sallis, 77
Salt Marsh Cottages, 84, 112
Salt Water Row, 110, 125
Sandfield Bridge, 143
Saul Brass Band, 107
Saunders, 113
Savings Bank; *see* Post Office Savings Bank
sawyer, 20, 30, 36, 108, 109
scabies, 144
scarlet fever, 119
school fees/pence, 25, 37, 64, 65, 70, 74, 82, 138
School House, The, 105
school inspector, 62, 64
School Lane, 105
School Row, 96, 97
schoolmaster, 15, 30, 41, 57, 62, 63, 65, 82, 99, 101, 105, 119, 121, 124
schoolmistress, 113, 138
schoolroom, 65, 66, 90, 115, 123, 124
scissors and knife grinder, 69
sculptor, 115, 118
Sea Fencibles, 118
seaman, 63, 69, 79
sempstress (seamstress), 33, 84, 126
Septennial Benefit Club, 36, 52, 74
servant, 8, 18, 29, 40, 54, 59, 69, 72, 76, 79, 82, 87, 108, 112, 114, 126, 129, 139
settlement, 107
Severn Bore, 14
Severn Estuary, 58
Severnthorpe, 119
sewing mistress, 62, 93, 143
sexton, 93
Shakespeare Cottage, 68
shepherd, 26, 72, 85
Shepherd's Cottage, The, 26
Shepherds, The, 26
ship owner, 53, 114
ship's carpenter, 63
shipwright, 143
shoemaker, 35, 41, 42, 51, 68, 111, 121
shopkeeper, 19, 106, 117
Shrubs, The, 61
Simpson, 55
skittle alley, 27
Small, 121
smallpox, 59, 62, 96, 132, 144
Smith, 34-5, 62-3, 95, 125, 126, 140
smokehouse, 46
soirées, 121, 127
soup kitchen, 24, 37, 54
Spire, 122
Splatt, 54, 85, 112
Splatt Bridge, 54, 84, 85, 86
Splatt Bridge House, 86
Splatt Cottages, 84
Splatt House, 81
Splatt Lane, 82, 83, 84
stableboy, 8
Stapleton, 15, 112
stationer and stamp distributor, 11, 90

staymaker, 33
steam dredger, 97
steam engine, 128, 145
steamer, 87
Stiff, 38-9, 111, 121
Stockelm Cottage, 10, 11, 12, 118
Stockham, 13, 106
stone mason; *see* mason
stone merchant, 54
Stonehouse Station, 18, 24
Stratford, 33
straw bonnet/hat maker, 35, 52
suicide, 43
Summer House, The, 56, 99, 100
Sumner, 11, 65, 67, 90
Sunday School, 51
Sunny Side, 39, 121
surgeon, 10, 36, 74, 108, 140, 144
Surveyor of the Highways, 81

tailor/taileress, 29, 100, 122, 125
tallow chandler, 44, 45, 117
Tamaris Cottage, 43
Tanfield, 80
Tanhouse Farm, 69, 80, 81, 82
tea meeting, 99, 102, 121, 124
teetotalism; *see* temperance
telegraph, 13, 82
temperance, 28, 124
Temperance Movement, 130
tenant farmer; *see* farmer
thatcher, 33, 85
Three Horseshoes, The, 40, 41, 46, 67, 113, 116, 117, 119
tile maker, 100
tinker, 69
Tom Clarke's Cottage, 39
Top O' the Green, 19, 37
Top Shop, The, 17
town crier, 52, 67
Townfield, 26, 60, 129
Townfield Farm, 101, 128
Transportation, 137
Tree Coffee House, 27, 75
Trigg, 137, 138, 139
Trillium, The, 41
trow, 29, 30, 58, 63, 72, 110
Truck Act 1887, 130
True Heart, The, 97, 121
Trueman, 38
Trustees of Roads, 57
Tudor Cottage, 49, 109
Tulip Cottage, 77, 105
Turner, 23, 27, 65, 78, 80, 126, 140
turnpike, 9, 18, 40
Turnpike, The, 127
turnpike toll collector, 127

vaccination, 96, 132
veterinary surgeon, 40, 67, 135
vicar, 14, 23, 24, 27, 28, 40, 46, 64, 65, 66, 67, 73-74, 76, 80, 89, 90, 91, 96, 99, 100, 107, 108, 123, 130, 138
Vicarage Coachhouse and Stables, 76
Vicarage Cottage, 75
Vicarage Lane, 67, 68, 70, 71, 75, 85
Vicarage, The, 13, 66, 73, 74

Vick, 108, 115
Vizard, 7, 22, 143

waggoner, 135
Walford House, 108, 113
Walham Brick Works, 81
Walk, 72
Walk Farm, 141
Walker, 127
Wallington, 7
Ward, 17, 42, 114-15
Wards Court, 42, 118
wash day, 15
watchmaker, 28
waterman, 20, 21, 41, 54, 58, 59, 60, 63, 68, 69, 77, 80, 82, 83, 85, 92, 94, 95, 97, 125, 143
Waters, 18, 145
Watery Lane, 37
Wathen, 83, 112
Watkins, 44, 117
Watts, 18, 36-7, 42, 52, 59, 65, 66, 74, 85, 86, 90, 107, 108, 119, 120, 131-2, 144-5
Wave, The, 87
waywarden, 15
weaver, 132, 138
Webb, 42, 100, 144
Wheatenhurst Highway District, 143
Wheatenhurst Union Workhouse, 26, 31, 40, 51
wheelwright; *see* carpenter and wheelwright
Wherrett, 36
White House, 30
White Lion Inn, Cambridge, 132
Whitminster Inn, 31, 99, 140, 143
Whitminster Lane, 40, 42, 54, 141
Whitminster Petty Sessions, 15, 31, 86, 95, 102, 144, 145
Whittard, 121
Whittle, 105
Whittles Lane, 104, 105
Wicks, 40, 91
Wicks Charity, 40
Wild Goose Cottage, 56, 58, 59
Wilkins, 40, 69, 83, 122
Wilks, 26, 33
Williams, 82
Winchcombe, 7, 103
Winter/Winters, 69, 81, 84-5, 86
Wisma Mulia, 144
Wood, 14, 66, 125
Woodbine Cottage, 50, 108, 109
Woodman, 59, 98
Woodward, 69, 92
wool picker, 17
Wooles, 49, 51, 104
woollen weaver; *see* weaver
workhouse, 10, 51, 55, 59, 118
Workman, 15, 80, 100, 118
Wotton, 47, 108, 145
Wright, 59, 92, 142, 143

Ye Olde Cruck House, 46
yellow fever, 144
Yew Tree Farm, 97
Yew Tree House, 54, 63
Young, 10, 11

R. Severn

Church

Gloucester and Berkeley Canal

53.

Parks
Farm